A beginner's guide to language and gender

MM Textbooks bring the subjects covered in our successful range of academic monographs to a student audience. The books in this series explore education and all aspects of language learning and use, as well as other topics of interest to students of these subjects. Written by experts in the field, the books are supervised by a team of world-leading scholars and evaluated by instructors before publication. Each text is student-focused, with suggestions for further reading and study questions leading to a deeper understanding of the subject.

Advisory Board

Professor Colin Baker, University of Wales, Bangor, UK

Professor Viv Edwards, University of Reading, Reading,UK

Professor Ofelia García, Columbia University, New York, USA

Dr Aneta Pavlenko, Temple University, Philadelphia, USA

Professor David Singleton, Trinity College, Dublin, Ireland

Professor Terrence G. Wiley, Arizona State University, Tempe, USA

For more details of this book or any other of our publications, please contact:

Multilingual Matters, Frankfurt Lodge, Clevedon Hall, Victoria Road, Clevedon, BS21 7HH, England.

http://www.multilingual-matters.com

MM Textbooks

Consultant Editor: Professor Viv Edwards

A beginner's guide to language and gender

Allyson Jule

Multilingual Matters Ltd

Clevedon · Buffalo · Toronto

Library of Congress Cataloging in Publication Data

Jule, Allyson
A Beginner's Guide to Language and Gender / Allyson Jule.
MM Textbooks
Includes bibliographical references and index.
1. Language and sex. I. Title.
P120.S48J85 2008
306.44-dc22   2007050430

British Library Cataloguing in Publication Data

A catalogue entry for this book is available from the British Library.

ISBN-13: 978-1-84769-056-2 (hbk)
ISBN-13: 978-1-84769-055-5 (pbk)

Multilingual Matters Ltd

UK: Frankfurt Lodge, Clevedon Hall, Victoria Road, Clevedon BS21 7HH.
USA: UTP, 2250 Military Road, Tonawanda, NY 14150, USA.
Canada: UTP, 5201 Dufferin Street, North York, Ontario M3H 5T8, Canada.

The policy of Multilingual Matters/Channel View Publications is to use papers
that are natural, renewable and recyclable products, made from wood grown in
sustainable forests. In the manufacturing process of our books, and to further
support our policy, preference is given to printers that have FSC and PEFC
Chain of Custody certification. The FSC and/or PEFC logos will appear on those
books where full certification has been granted to the printer concerned.

Printed and bound in Great Britain by the Cromwell Press Ltd.

*Dedicated to my children, Clark and Jane, who
very helpfully transcend many gender classifications
and, as a direct result, are constant fascinations
and inspirations.*

Contents

Acknowledgments

My heartfelt gratitude goes to so many people who helped make this book a reality, especially Viv Edwards and everyone at Multilingual Matters for the support and encouragement through the final stages of going to print. I am also very grateful to Judith Baxter for her thoughtful comments on the manuscript itself and for the addition of her insightful preface to the book. I am so thankful for Cheryl Wall and her tenacious friendship and keyboarding skills extraordinaire, as well as for Kate Power and her thorough and helpful review of the book in draft form. Also, the inclusion of me by the members of IGALA, the International Gender and Language Association, has meant a great deal to me over the years. I am grateful for the many ways they have engaged with my ideas. A special thanks also goes to my students who have helped form the ideas presented here. Most intimately, I wish to thank my family for their support and generosity in giving me the time, space and places to think.

Preface

One of the most exciting and popular subjects to emerge in recent years from the larger field of sociolinguistics is gender and language. Associated with 'second wave' feminism in the early 1970s, gender and language has now shifted its primary focus from the study of 'femininities' to gendered identities in general. In many ways, its value today stems from asking students to consider the obvious: a world that has taken the social categories of sex and gender to be highly meaningful in constructing who we are, how we should speak and how we should represent ourselves in everyday life. Most of us have experienced the feeling of being pigeonholed as 'female' or 'male' by something we have said or done. At times, this can be liberating and at other times, limiting and debilitating. Gender and language provides us with a critical lens by which to view the way language shapes our identities as gendered people. It offers us a means of challenging limiting and unfair stereotypes and perhaps redefining who we are.

Despite the popularity of gender and language, there are as yet very few books that help students to assimilate this complex and burgeoning field of study. This engaging handbook by Allyson Jule shows that gender and language is equally about our personal and lived experience as it is about different scholarly perspectives and theories. It shows that acting out our lives as gendered people implicates all aspects of our selves: as students, partners, parents, workers, friends, worshippers, entertainers and consumers of culture. The book provides a guide through the subject's historical origins, key theoretical perspectives and latest thinking in the field. It also invites readers to consider how gender and language influences education, the workplace, the media, religion and a range of interpersonal and social contexts.

The book is clear in proposing that there is still a political agenda to meet. In many parts of the world, language remains a means of oppression in ensuring that women in particular do not share power on equal terms with men. This book reminds us that if we can make hidden assumptions about gender and language more explicit, we are playing our part in making this world a better place to live as scholars and as human beings.

Judith Baxter
University of Reading, UK

Part 1:
Understanding gender and language use

1

The emergence of gender and language study

This chapter explores some of the complexities of studying gender and language use by asking key questions:

- Why study gender and language use?

- Why do some social scientists see 'sex' and 'gender' as distinct terms? And does the distinction matter?

- How has feminism contributed as a social and political movement in the West to the field of gender and language studies?

- Why is it important to understand all people of all ages and all cultures as gendered – and not just women or just boys?

- What is sexist language and how is it used to 'genderize' ourselves and others?

- And finally, how is our use of language both a mirror that reflects our views, attitudes and beliefs, and a tool for change?

'Feminism is the radical notion that women are people.'
Cheris Kramarae, Paula Treichler and Ann Russo (*A Feminist Dictionary*, 1996)

I have been interested in **gender roles** for a long time, probably since I was born. I grew up with an older brother and sister and, like all of us, my early life was heavily influenced by my **gender**. I had a pink bedroom and was absolutely delighted to receive Barbie dolls for Christmas. My mother was a nurse, a good cook and an attentive housekeeper; my father 'went to work', mowed the grass and took care of the car. In short, I grew up with stereotypical gender roles around me and, until I came to recognize the limitations of these gender distinctions, I saw gender as unproblematic. After all, I liked Barbie dolls – as did my sister but not my brother. We felt no oppression. My life goal to be a language teacher seemed very possible and realistic and, without too much effort, I qualified as a teacher in due course. In many ways, I am a 'typical' woman: I am married, I have children, I like to bake and to read, and I cry quite easily too.

So why on earth am I (or anyone) writing a handbook on gender and language use? There are two reasons. One is that being rehearsed into gender performances predicts life choices like mine. This relationship between socialization and individual identity is reason enough to consider the complexities and implications of gender in our lives. The second reason is that the rehearsal into genderedness is most fascinatingly revealed in the way we speak. My particular fascination in the relationship of gender and language use emerged from my early experiences as a classroom language teacher: quickly I noticed that the young men and young women in my classrooms had quite different classroom experiences and distinct opportunities for learning because of their gender roles. These realizations promoted my lifelong curiosity about the effects of language on one's gender as well as the influence gender has on the ways we speak.

One example of **gendered** tendencies as expressed in language use is the way I have begun to write this book. I have already used a gendered tendency by using personal anecdote. This is the writing **voice** I am most comfortable to write in. Apparently this personal revelation/conversational style is something understood by my society as **feminine**, because it is understood as accessible and relational. This style might serve my purposes here quite well – to draw you in; or it might limit my authority by undermining the legitimacy of what I might have to say. Either way, my gender and its connection with you matters a great deal to my message: how I speak reveals my gendered tendencies as well as rehearses me in them further. Also, your reaction to my style tells us something about you, too. Those with a more feminine communicative style may find my way of communicating engaging while those with more experience with **masculine** discourse may find this personal touch disconcerting. However, these claims are tricky to support because of the assumptions embedded in them.

For the last ten years at least, there has been an equal interest in masculinities as well as femininities and in the gender continuum that links them. Language and gender study is for both sexes because it questions how gender is represented and constructed. More even power relations can be achieved by asking both sexes to be critical of both traditional and contemporary gender identities. Both Robert Connell (1995) as well as Martin Mac an Ghaill (2000) focus their research on the various expressions of current masculinity. Also, although this book is not about sexuality and sexual identity *per se*, language and sexuality are also closely linked and integral to the field.

In this book, I seek to introduce you to the sociolinguistic field of gender; that is to say, this book introduces you to sociolinguistics as a field of study that is sometimes concerned with the use of language (both its powers and its limitations) through and with the lens of gender that includes an understanding that all people are gendered. My hope is that, as a beginner's handbook, the ideas here will be accessible as well as engaging for you and inspire you to continue to explore and reflect on the ways gender impacts on our communication. Gender is a major part of who we are and why we behave in certain ways. As such, it is worthwhile to consider the many ways our gender identity influences how we live our lives. Social scientists have been curious about such things for a very long time. May the ideas in this book help to orientate you to one of the most dynamic fields of the social sciences. Also, this book includes a glossary of key terms. As you see certain words or phrases like this, you can refer to the glossary for relevant definitions.

Sex and gender:
an important distinction

Important to mention at the very beginning is what gender is understood to be and how it is distinct from sex. Though the words are often used interchangeably, they mean quite different things to social scientists. Some scholars see sex as determined by our being born male or female, and it has far-reaching consequences for us as individuals. Biological sex affects how we experience our lives and how we act in the world. In this view, sex is related to gender but it is not the same thing. Gender concerns the social category of behavior. It is strongly associated with the social divisions made on the basis of sex, and language plays a major role in establishing and sustaining these divisions. Though the word 'gender' is a grammatical category in some languages (such as the 'masculine' or 'feminine' used for syntactic meaning in French or Italian), the social sciences use gender as a social category where masculine and feminine are understood to be behavioral categories usually ascribed to and aligned with those born with the correlative sex. Thus, individuals who are born male are expected to display behaviors that are perceived and understood by our society as masculine, and those born female are associated with behaviors that are perceived and understood as feminine by those in her family, her school, her neighborhood and the larger culture surrounding her.

Some scholars have questioned this distinction, particularly in light of the burgeoning literature on sexuality and sexual identities. While this book is not primarily about this, language and sexuality are clearly linked. Deborah Cameron (2005) has been particularly vocal about the role of language and sexuality; as have Mary Bucholtz and Kira Hall (2004).

The distinction between sex and gender was first articulated in detail by a British feminist in the early 1970s. It was Anne Oakley (1972) who defined sex as biologically based, a matter of physiology, something related to genes, gonads, hormones and anatomy. The female ova contain the female sex chromosome X; a male sperm contains either X or Y chromosomes. Whether we are born male or female is determined by our biological father giving either an X or a Y chromosome. Except in unusual circumstances, sex is essentially binary: one is *either* male *or* female.

Gender, by contrast, is **socially constructed**: it is something we learn. Social scientists believe that we acquire social characteristics and engage in behaviors because of how we are understood by those around us. Simone de Beauvoir (1952) believed that we gradually become masculine or feminine and we behave in gendered ways in a whole variety of circumstances for a host of reasons. Unlike sex, gender is not binary; we are not masculine *or* feminine. Instead, we are a combination of many characteristics that could be understood as either or both masculine or feminine depending on the context and our relationships with those involved. It is possible to say someone is 'more masculine' or 'more feminine' – for example, we can say someone is 'very manly' or 'such a girl', but rarely do we say one is 'maler' or 'femaler'. We act out gender roles from a continuum of masculine and feminine characteristics; we are therefore gendered and we are involved in the process of our own gendering and the gendering of others throughout our lives. In the field of gender and language use, this performance of gender is referred to as 'doing gender'. In many ways we are rehearsed into our gender roles, like being prepared for a part in a play: gender is something we do, not something we are (Bergvall, 1999; Butler, 1990). Over our lives and particularly in our early formative years, we are conditioned, prompted and prodded to behave in acceptable ways so that our gender, and our community's understanding of it, aligns with our ascribed sex.

Though some scholars in the field question the distinction that sex is a biological property and gender is a cultural construct, and both terms continue to be contested, I hold to the distinction for the sake of clarity.

Nowadays, the process of 'doing gender' is something that begins even before birth and may be on a fixed course that is difficult to interrupt. Many new parents know the sex of their baby months before the baby is born, and thus they begin to associate certain gender characteristics with their baby: they buy pink clothes for a baby girl and blue clothes for a baby boy; they imagine particular experiences as possible or impossible because of their baby's sex; some people even have preferences for one sex over the other and may abort if the baby is not of the desired sex. Whether the differences between boys and girls and then men and women are innate or socialized (or both), we are distinguished by the differences.

Throughout infancy, early childhood, the school-years, adolescence, early adulthood and even into middle age and as seniors, we are responded to based on our sex and our gender performance. Likewise, we respond to others based on their sex/gender relationship. In both respects, we are gendered. If gender was exclusively a matter of one's biological sex, we would always see the same displays of gender roles and behaviors across all cultures, across all time periods and across all age groups, but we do not. There is extraordinary diversity. The way my mother performed her gender as a young woman in the 1950s is quite different from the way I behaved, felt, spoke as a young woman in the 1980s, and this performance of gender is different again from my daughter's genderedness as a young woman in the 21st century. We have different tastes, expectations and life experiences that are linked to the gender worlds of our particular generation. Also, a woman of my similar age but living in a dramatically different culture (say, in the Congo) will have a different set of possible life experiences to mine. Gender performances are not universal, but gender as a social construct is a universal factor influencing the way people live their lives and understand each other.

It is the extent to which behavior is biologically determined and/or learned through social experiences that is the tricky part. Are there behaviors that can be attributed solely to our biological sex? Which arise from our gender? Some gender roles are fairly straightforward; for example, women bear children so are in a special position to be mothers. But other roles are not sex-based and are not roles as much as they are positions played out in context. For example, both men and women can soothe a crying child and be a valuable nurturer. Some scholars, such as Judith Butler (1990), do not make the sex/gender distinction so central; instead, they see both sex and gender as socially constructed. A worthwhile discussion on the complexity of separating sex and gender can be found in Deborah Cameron's (2005) writing on the subject.

Mary Talbot's (1998) work cautions us against simply mapping gender onto sex and casting all behavior presented by boys and men as masculine and all behavior presented by girls and women as feminine. Talbot suggests, and I agree, that doing so limits our full humanity. Mapping gender onto sex comes from an assumption that 'socially determined differences between women and men are natural and inevitable' (p. 9). Viewing sex and gender as the same thing often connects to the promotion of traditional, conservative family roles and to the justifications for male privilege and power that align with these roles. Simplifying gender to merge with biology permits and can even promote certain behaviors. Such thinking is known as **biological determinism**. With this view, we can say things such as 'women are like that' and dismiss something more complex about being human and about understanding our human experience as more mysterious and complicated. If the distinction between sex and gender is blurred or completely erased so that sex is seen as the same as gender, then certain restrictions and demands can be placed on us as women and men. 'Women are like that' becomes 'women should be like that' or 'men don't ask for directions' becomes 'men should never ask for help'. Such sentiments become belief and support a binary, polarized understanding of men and women.

Biological determinism is also linked to **essentialism**. An essentialist view of gender tries to establish and affirm a genetic basis for our behaviors and life trajectories. Racial views can also fall victim to this kind of thinking; for example, a belief that Blacks are musical because it's 'in their blood'. Obviously, this is a stereotype; some Blacks are musical but certainly not all. Besides, some Black culture values and promotes music so how can we separate the culture from the individual? However, some radical feminists hold to biological determinism as an explanation of gendered differences, such as Andrea Dworkin (1981: 515) who said 'Violence is male and the male is the penis'. To her, being male equates with being violent. It is 'in their blood' to commit certain crimes (such as rape) or to enjoy the power of their position of observer as experienced in pornography, for example. Perhaps more men than women do commit rape as well as look at pornography, but this does not imply that *all* men would do so simply by virtue of their having penises, or that women are incapable of similar violence. I think Dworkin's line of thinking can be problematic because it can undermine our ability to create meaningful and authentic lives: it can narrow what is possible and serve as a trap around us. Biology plays a major part in forming our possible life experiences, but the ways we are responded to throughout our lives and the ways we are socially constructed by those around us are perhaps more influential. I think it is helpful to hold a *both/and* view of gender and sex rather than an *either/or*.

The problem with any essentialist view is that the attempt to simplify undermines what is infinitely complex and unique to each person. For any claim by biological determinists or essentialists, such as 'girls are better at languages', there is a counterclaim, such as 'boys are better at speaking aloud'. Some scholars, such as Deborah Cameron (2005), suggest that studies of difference between the sexes ultimately have a political dimension. Why do we want to find differences? Whose purposes are being served by such inquiry? One's understanding of gender often aligns with larger political or philosophical views: those who see gender as working on a complex continuum do not limit people based on their sex, whereas those who see gender as fixed and biologically determined run the risk of limiting the human experience to restricted gender roles and demands for both women and men. In addition, the particular way we use words both reflects and reinforces our attitudes to gender, and in many ways it is the main way by which we construct gendered attitudes.

The rise of feminism: a quick review

The study of gender and language emerges from feminist thought. The Oxford English Dictionary defines feminism as 'the policy, practice, or advocacy of the political, economic, and social equality for women'. This definition is helpful enough, but there are strong connotations around the issue of feminism that a dictionary definition cannot adequately explore. Today's feminism is a diverse phenomenon with a long and painful history with a starting point that may be impossible to locate. The current field includes three main camps, each with a differing perspective on the relationship between female oppression and <u>patriarchy</u>:

1. **liberal feminism** seeks primarily to watch and comment on society's view of women as indicative of society's patriarchal attitudes and values, particularly regarding laws and human rights;
2. **socialist feminism** sees patriarchy alongside social class issues of dominance and power; and
3. **radical feminism** focuses on patriarchy as male dominance over women and challenges society to examine, challenge and dismantle it.

Other variations of feminism include psychoanalytic feminism, existentialist feminism, post-modern feminism, Islamic feminism, Jewish feminism, Christian feminism and post-structural feminism – each of which focuses on the female experience in society. The study of gendered language often connects with liberal feminist ideas because of the shared concern for women in particular as victims of a patriarchal system. Though there has been recent focus on masculinities and men as well as on gay and lesbian communities, the field of gender and language has been predominantly focused on women and how they 'lose out' by contemporary constructions of gender.

Most feminists believe that all societies have been and still are patriarchal and that males and the male experience define what it is to be human, including what it means to be female. The female has been treated as **the other** whose existence is defined and interpreted by those who are male. Feminists believe it is important to understand and study gender as a system of cultural signs, often assigned to two distinct body forms: male and female. For feminists, it is critical that we demystify and subvert the power-based relationships attached to gender so that both women and men might live more freely.

Feminism is usually a bedrock in women's studies or gender studies within academia, but it is also a specialty area of its own that contributes to various disciplines including education, fine arts, the humanities, and to all the social sciences, including anthropology, linguistics, philosophy, communications and psychology. There are a multitude of ways in which feminism intersects with academic discussions. Some feminist scholars explore gendered ways of speaking, learning, thinking, writing, counseling; while others explore gender-specific health and medical concerns, family and domestic realities or tensions, and legal rights or access to representation. There are also feminist researchers focused on the 'rewriting' of history to incorporate neglected aspects of female experience and perspective. Some scholars examine literary theory and the ways in which women and women's lives are depicted in literature and art, as well as the ways in which literature and language are created by genderedness.

For students encountering academic feminisms for the first time, it is important to be aware that the term 'feminist' is not as politically loaded in academia as it is sometimes understood to be in society more generally. Indeed, a single, common accepted academic definition of feminism is hard to find. 'Feminisms' (plural), in fact, may be a better word choice and is often preferred by feminist scholars because it more adequately reflects the diversity of their work. All of the varieties of feminisms do, however, represent critiques of patriarchy or critiques of <u>misogyny</u> to some extent. It may also be safe to say that all feminisms express some form of disenchantment with our <u>androcentric</u> society, a society that sees the male experience as the central point of reference, <u>the norm</u>, while the female experience is marked, different and regarded as something other.

There are countless examples of how patriarchy is revealed in our language use. Take, for example, the word 'waiter' as the perceived norm or the unmarked word used in our everyday language, while 'waitress' is the linguistically marked variation. The use of the word 'waitress' highlights the server as being of the female sex, while the word 'waiter' is the starting point. The highlighting of otherness is what is meant by 'marked'. You can no doubt think of similar examples (actor/actress; air host/hostess) as well as ways in which such gendered terms have begun to change to the gender-neutral (flight attendant). Similar biases exist in academic work. Most developmental psychology, for example, has been based on the male experience, thus privileging the male experience as the norm. Feminist scholars are concerned with the ways these kinds of assumptions function in society and how they can be exposed, examined and interrupted for reasons of accountability and justice. Feminisms explore whose voices and stories get heard in society, including in politics, business, academia, classrooms, churches and families. All feminists, in every field, are focused on such questions and the many possible complex answers.

Waves of feminism

Feminism is most often understood as happening in three waves: first, second and third. These movements are helpfully described by many feminist scholars, including Sara Mills (1995) and Judith Baxter (2003). The first wave of feminism is feminism before women could vote and its cause and focus was the practical emancipation of women. Second wave feminism is the mid-20th-century concern for equal pay for equal work, while third wave feminism emerges in the 1980s as identity feminism and concerning personal choice issues.

Especially in the later half of the 20th century, feminism became characterized by major American movements such as the **Equal Rights Amendment** and the **National Organization of Women (**NOW**)**. These American incarnations of feminism insisted that women should be free to pursue independent careers and economic independence, as well as to have freedom from any male-based oppression in their personal relationships. However, this particular second wave of American feminism took off in the 1960s, following the heavily domestic focus of a 1950s post-war America. It was a uniquely potent era for the realignment of all social roles, including and perhaps especially gender roles. Feminism in the 1960s was particularly focused on **consciousness raising groups** where women together began to question and reject the role of housewife that was so entrenched in America at the time. These **baby-boomers** ushered in an unprecedented revolution regarding social roles, politics, religion, affluence, philosophy and the politics of war and peace. The American feminism of the 1960s was among a whole plethora of movements and social challenges to authority at the time, such as the anti-war movement and the civil rights movement. The sexual revolution of the 1960s attacked traditional models of male–female relationships and sought to establish new, more **egalitarian** patterns of behavior.

By the 1970s and 1980s, Western society saw many legal reforms, such as more equal pay for equal work, more accessible divorce laws, some access to legal abortion, increased day care regulations and funding, and more affirmative action in the workplace and educational institutions. However, while the issue of women's marginalization from power entered Western social consciousness in a particularly influential manner in the 1960s, leading to significant changes in the workforce, university programs, the literary canon and family dynamics, it is important to understand that feminism as a concept is much older than the 1960s and infinitely more complex and fluid. Indeed, the study of, and concern for, women and women's experiences reaches far back and embraces all cultures all over the world.

Sappho, an ancient poet from the 8th century CE, as well as many medieval mystics such as Hildegard of Bingen (1098–1179 CE), Julian of Norwich (1342–1416 CE) and the 17th-century writer Aphra Behn (1640–89 CE), set the stage to an enlightened perspective on life and society as well as a feminist version of truth and experience. Major feminist thinkers include England's Mary Wollstonecraft who wrote *A Vindication of the Rights of Woman* in 1792. Wollstonecraft criticized the lack of rigorous education for girls in 18th-century England and their weaker positions in society as a direct result of poor education. She believed that women were not able to hold positions of power because they lacked the training necessary to do so; as such, it was imperative that society educate its women and equip them to participate outside their domestic roles.

American activist, Sarah Moore Grimke, wrote *Letters on the Equality of the Sexes* in the early 1800s. In 1843, Sojourner Truth gave her 'Ain't I a Woman?' speech as part of the anti-slavery movement in the US. Elizabeth Cady Stanton wrote *The Woman's Bible* in 1895, a document offering a woman's perspective on Biblical events. There were also various writers from the Women's Christian Temperance Movement who established the Young Women's Christian Association and influenced major prison reforms throughout the British Empire, including Australia, New Zealand and Canada. Britain's Emmeline Pankhurst and her universal suffrage movement gave the vote to all British women, extending throughout the British Empire. Virginia Woolf's feminist lectures to Cambridge's Girton Women's College compiled in *A Room of One's Own* was published in 1928. There were also women who focused attention on women's service and experience in the two world wars and between the wars, including the flappers in the jazz age and the Depression era reforms led by Eleanore Roosevelt. France's Simone de Beauvoir wrote *The Second Sex* in 1949 (translated into English in 1952).

All these women and a host of many others were established as major world writers, thinkers and politicians long before the popularized American feminists such as Betty Freidan and Gloria Steinem (and Germaine Greer in the UK) championed feminism for white, upper middle class, suburban American women. Feminism has been, and continues to be, the effort to make life fair for everyone, to dismantle gender roles that limit both genders, and to interrupt gender stereotyping.

It is critical to recognize that the study of gender and language use emerges from the ideas promoted in previous generations, and that the growth in a feminist consciousness is woven into our shared history and is foundational to the study of gender and language use. Both patriarchy and feminism have involved shifts in perspectives and understanding from within the social sciences and the humanities. The issue of sex and gender is more complex and far-reaching than any of us can grasp because it is wrapped by the billions of individual lives influencing the female experience as well as the male experience. We are all gendered, not just women.

Of concern to us here in this book is the relationship of gender and language use. In the early part of the 20th-century, the patriarchal system entrenched in Western society could easily be seen in the sociolinguistic writings at the time, particularly in the influential work of Otto Jespersen (1922). Early on, this Danish linguist set the stage by suggesting that women spoke in ways different from men because they were unable to speak in strong, coherent sentences or with an extensive vocabulary. He believed that the greatest orators of history were always and only men because of innate abilities in men that were rarely (if ever) found in women. Many at that time agreed with him. However, there were also others who had different perspectives. For example, Virginia Woolf (1928) in *A Room of One's Own* suggested that women's absence from positions of real world power had to do with the lack of opportunity and the lack of adequate training available for women and not because those born female were inherently unable to be innovative or sophisticated in thought and language. Other sexist views persisted that feminists began to critique, starting with **sexism** in the language itself.

Sexist language

Sexism as a term was coined in the 1960s, along with the term **racism**, to describe discrimination in society based on certain personal traits, such as being born female or male or being born black or white. Sexism helps identify the historical patriarchal **hierarchy** that has existed between men and women where one (man) is considered the norm and the other (woman) is marked as other – as something quite different from the norm. In this view, the other can be exploited, manipulated, constrained or even adored and made remote because of their difference from what is considered the usual experience. In gender studies, this **othering** is usually associated with women, but it can be also based on other personal features, such as race, religion, sexual orientation or disabilities – anything that is viewed as different from the perceived norm.

Questions and criticisms of sexist language have emerged because of a concern that language is a powerful medium through which the world is both reflected and constructed. One example of **gender bias** in language use is the case of pronouns, particularly the generic use of 'he' or 'him' to refer to something relating to both men and women. Feminist linguists, such as Dale Spender (1990), believe that language has been historically man-made with the male forms reflecting the male's position in society and the female forms perceived as deviant. Some have claimed that the use of generics (such as 'mankind' to refer to both men and women) reinforces a binary that sees the male and masculine as the norm and the female and feminine as the 'not norm'. Such lexical markings are also understood to have prevented women from expressing and raising consciousness about their own experiences as legitimately human by preventing women from speaking with their own voice (Gilligan, 1982). Their invisibility in language and associated silence perpetuates gender assumptions in society, so that we come to see what is male and experienced by those who are male as the only point of reference; by contrast, we see what is female and experienced by those who are female as a variation (but not the primary example) of human experience. It is this kind of injustice that has fueled much feminist scholarship.

Sexist language also presents stereotypes of both females and males, sometimes to the disadvantage of males, but more often to the disadvantage of females. This sexism is seen universally in all languages. In English, Robin Lakoff (1975) uses the example of 'master' vs 'mistress' to make the point: there are unequal connotations that surround these two matching terms – and to the detriment of those born female – 'Master' has strong and powerful connotations, while 'mistress' does not. Feminists have also objected to the use of generic expressions because of what cannot be truly generic. We might be able to say, 'Man is a lonely creature' but we cannot say, 'Man has difficulty in childbirth' because one is universal while the other is not. As such, generics too often assume too much and reinforce patriarchy as a result. David Graddol and Joan Swann (1989) have written on sexist language and how sexist expressions limit our understanding of the human experience by always seeing the lived experience through a gendered lens. Other examples of 'woman doctor' or 'male nurse' qualify the adjective, making it different and reinforcing a tendency to see certain tasks in society as aligned with assumed gender roles.

Sexist language also includes the depiction of women in the position of passive object rather than active subject, such as on the basis of their appearance ('a blonde') or domestic roles ('a mother of two') when similar depictions in similar contexts would not be made of men. These representations of women trivialize their lives and place an extra level of personal judgment on them. Men can be trivialized and negatively judged by sexist language as well (such as, 'what a stud') but feminists often argue that the connotations in such examples are not as severe and not as limiting in the same way as they are for women. Indeed, viewing a man as an object of desire may be understood by both men and women as flirtatious, affirming and even desirable. Our shared patriarchal history means that the connotations cannot be the same.

Ultimately, feminist linguists hope that attention given to language will denaturalize the assumed male privilege, along with the patriarchal system that secures it, and loosen gender roles for both males and females. But sexist language is not only located in the content or meanings of specific words or phrases. It can also be found in dialogue, in our conversations and in the meanings and communication created by our speech styles or patterns. Language changes from one context to another, from one community to another and from one time period to another. Language changes as a result of social, political and economic processes. It changes because of lifestyle changes and encounters with technologies and media and migration. That sometimes I speak in a more informal way aligns with my hopes and intentions.

Language can be used as a vehicle for social change but it also reflects present attitudes and views and is no small matter for sociolinguists. Language use reveals our awareness or lack of awareness of human complexity, whether spoken, written, visual or multi-modal. While the most obvious function of language is to communicate information, language also contributes to two other equally important functions. One is to express and create social identity and the other is to establish and maintain social relationships. These functions may be recognized less often because gender is conveyed not so much through *what* we say as through *how* we say it.

Gendered language was not taken as a serious topic of study until the 1960s, and it did not develop as a subfield in its own right until the publication of Robin Lakoff's book, *Language and Woman's Place* in 1975. A feminist work, Lakoff's book presented impressionistic conclusions regarding the speech of heterosexual, white, middle-class American women, in the form what she calls 'woman's language'. Lakoff argued that women use particular language features because they are denied means of strong expression within a male-dominated society.

Many studies following Lakoff's work also focused on heterosexual, white, middle-class women, and many of these accepted and agreed with Lakoff's observations and conclusions about gendered language use. Other explanations, however, also began to emerge. For example, Deborah Tannen's work in the 1990s argued that gender differences are parallel to cross-cultural differences. She claimed that men and women rely on different subcultural norms when interpreting cultural information encoded by language use. She suggested, for example, that female-based subcultures often use language to build personal relationships over the creation of hierarchical relationships. For Tannen, the differences in language use between women and men result from the intent or purpose and not from the dominant position of men in society.

In the 1990s, the study of the relationship between gender and language moved toward viewing language as performative of gender identity and not simply reflective of it: people were seen to create gender through their own speech and to do so in a variety of ways. Penelope Eckert (1989), for example, argued that the language used in a Detroit high school created a limited selection of social identities for female students (such as 'girl' or 'white') because other self-definitions (such as being a star athlete) were socially unavailable to girls. Gender and language scholars began to see gender as a chosen performance – as a way of coping with ascribed gender roles within particular communities. Mary Talbot (1998), for instance, took a strong view of language and gender, suggesting that the use of language creates gender distinctions, rather than simply reflecting them. She used the phrase 'language-as-mirror' to describe how language reveals our thoughts and attitudes. Calling a grown woman 'girl', displays the particular social attitude toward women that sees women as less threatening when childlike. In such ways there is more to the language than what is said.

This chapter has introduced you to the study of gender and language and the various ways feminism has influenced sociolinguistics as well as the contested distinction of male/female and masculine/feminine. Our gendered identities, whether innate or socially constructed, propel our participation in society in a myriad of ways. What we consider universal or idiosyncratic influences our understanding of gender in our daily interactions with those around us. What we say and what is said to us are greatly affected by our gender.

Summary statements	
	• Feminism can be defined as the policy, practice or advocacy of the political, economic and social equality for women, but it has a long history and a complicated relationship with society.
	• Our sex is determined by our being born male or female, while gender is a complex and fluid social category of behaviors often associated with our biological sex but not necessarily, and is hugely questionable.
	• The relationship of sexism to language use is especially powerful because of the way language use reflects, promotes and legitimates certain attitudes and beliefs.

With a partner or on your own, consider:

1. If gender performances are not universal, how can it be that gender is a universal ingredient influencing the way we live our lives? Explain with examples from your own life.

2. Why is it important to recognize the history of feminism? Does it matter that each generation has its own particular issues to explore? What are some of this generation's unique issues?

3. In what ways does your language use align with your gender identity?

Further reading

To read more on the field of gender and language study, see:

Butler, J. (1990) *Gender Trouble: Feminism and the Subversion of Identity.* London: Routledge.

Cameron, D. and Kulick, D. (2003) *Language and Sexuality.* Cambridge: Cambridge University Press

Christie, C. (2000) *Gender and Language.* Edinburgh: Edinburgh University Press.

Coates, J. (2004) *Women, Men and Language* (3rd edn). New York: Pearson.

Crawford, M. (1995) *Talking Difference: On Gender and Language.* London: Sage.

Eckert, P. and McConnell-Ginet, S. (2003) *Language and Gender.* Cambridge: Cambridge University Press.

Gilligan, C. (1982) *In a Different Voice: Psychological Theory and Women's Development.* Cambridge, MA: Harvard University Press.

Goddard, A. and Patterson, L. (2000) *Language and Gender.* London: Routledge.

Holmes, J. and Meyerhoff, M. (2003) *The Handbook of Language and Gender.* Oxford: Blackwell.

Marchbank, J. and Leatherby, G. (2007) *Introduction to Gender: Social Science Perspectives.* Harlow: Pearson Longman.

Sunderland, J. (2004) *Gendered Discourses.* Basingstoke: Palgrave Macmillan.

Sunderland, J. (2006) *Language and Gender: An Advanced Resource Book.* London: Routledge.

Talbot, M. (1998) *Language and Gender: An Introduction.* Cambridge: Polity Press.

2

Language as gendered

This chapter explores the complexities of language as a gendered system by asking these key questions:

- How does language use reflect, create and sustain gender identity?

- Traditionally, why has the view of women's language use aligned with weakness while men's language use aligned with authority? Why is the very assumption that there are gendered ways of speaking problematic?

- What was known as 'women's language' and why has the phrase and its focus become less relevant?

- What are 'deficit/dominance theory' and 'difference theory' and how do these views influence the study of gender and language?

- How does our gender identity align with our use of language? Is gender one variable among many or is it the main influence on our language patterns?

- In what ways is Critical Discourse Analysis (CDA) used to examine language use? Are there other methods?

'One is not born a woman, one becomes a woman.'
Simone de Beauvoir (*The Second Sex*, 1949)

Two of the lingering tensions in understanding gender and language are how language use reflects our attitudes concerning men and women and how language creates our attitudes toward gender roles and expectations. Consider how women in various work settings are frequently subordinate in relation to men in those same workplaces. Or consider the way in which women are sometimes addressed in public discourse as 'girl' (such as, 'We have a new girl at the office') whereas men are rarely referred to as 'boy' in a similar context. This chapter highlights key ways in which our language use is understood to be both gendered and active in gendering our perceptions.

Early in the 20th century, the American linguists and anthropologists, Edward Sapir and Benjamin Whorf (Sapir, 1929), declared that 'the limits of one's language *are* the limits of one's world'. This is known as the **Sapir–Whorf hypothesis** – that there is a systemic relationship between a person's language use and how s/he understands the world. This hypothesis (also referred to as linguistic determinism) suggests that language use reveals our experiences and cannot be beyond our experiences: language cannot transcend us. But current researchers are increasingly critical of this stance. Even though we might not have a word for a certain notion or feeling, this does not mean we cannot experience it. For example, a woman in the 19th century might well have experienced 'domestic abuse' before such a term existed. In fact, her experience might well have contributed to the development of the term. In view of this, it seems reasonable to connect language with more creative and idiosyncratic possibilities – that language use is something highly artistic, imaginative and ever-changing. Some may use the term 'girl', for example, in an ironic fashion, to express a more sophisticated understanding of power relations and an awareness of society as stubbornly patriarchal, rather than earlier, dismissive views of what it means to be female. The way we speak reflects so much about what we are, but the reasons behind our language choices can be problematic.

To view language only as reflective suggests that we are limited in our power to change social realities – that we can only express what we experience and that we can only experience what we have words for. However, we *can* and *do* use language to change attitudes; we can also change our public understandings of our own realities often and throughout our lives. Language use has a lot to do with this. Studying language and gender is closely related to feminist concerns to stop the reproduction of systematic inequalities between men and women, and it is also related to identifying ways we speak in everyday moments. Language plays a complex part in reflecting and creating genderedness. The study of language can also play a big part in changing gender divisions while it busies itself revealing them. It is therefore worth considering the view of the feminine as deficient and the masculine as powerful in order to understand any possible alternative understandings. If we understand where we have been, we can have a better understanding of where we are and where we might go from here.

There have been many sociolinguistic studies that have claimed group differences in the way language is used by women and by men: namely that across social classes, ethnic groupings and age groups, women consistently use more linguistic features associated with standard language. These studies use what is known as the variationist perspective. Perhaps the best-known work of this type was done by the American William Labov (1966), who explored the notion of linguistic change, the type of study of which is known as variationist sociolinguistics. His studies on language change were attempts to understand different demographic groups, which ultimately led him to claim that men speak with more variation, more vernacularly (casually) than women do. This observation led to the view that men are more at ease in their social settings (that they are freer to adjust to situations), and that women are more anxious and less at ease in social situations because of their need to achieve or maintain social status. Alternatively, women use more standard language because doing so grants them access to legitimacy; alternatively, men are freer to be creative with language because they are already 'legitimate'. Of course, others disagreed with this interpretation, suggesting instead that gender-based linguistic differences arise from the fact that women are more concerned with others than men are and therefore more often choose standard language forms, which are more inclusive of others.

Peter Trudgill (1974) conducted a survey in Norwich, England, modeled on Labov's New York study, attempting to establish the variation of formality along gender lines. However, Trudgill found that women claimed to use more standard speech than they actually did, while men claimed to use more vernacular speech than they actually did. In response, Trudgill suggested that, rather than reflecting actual speech patterns, perceived differences may be the result of social attitudes about the acceptable behavior of women and men. In other words, since we already believe women to be more status-conscious than men, we interpret their speech patterns this way. But why would we do this? One explanation involves our view of women's social position: we believe that women need to secure and maintain social status, and that they use language as a means of doing so. Another explanation derives from our appraisal of men in terms of their occupation or earning power: we do not regard men as using standard or formal language to secure their social position, because it is already relatively secure. In general, we are more likely to think of men as being more autonomous, and women as more supportive of others. Consequently, this is what we tend to see when we analyze their speech.

Women's language and the language of power

For new scholars to the field, it is important to be aware that there are two ways to define, analyze, and interpret language use in alignment with gender: the **theory of deficit or dominance** and the **theory of difference**. The first understands any gender differences in language use as a result of women being dominated by men in various interactions. The second is the view that women and men are distinguished by their differences; that they belong to distinct subcultures that are benignly different. (No one is oppressed and no one is the oppressor.) Both of these views reflect the political climate at their particular time of popularity.

The deficit/dominance view

When Robin Lakoff first published her influential account of women's language, *Language and Woman's Place*, in 1975, she established a set of basic assumptions about the language of women. Among her claims are that females:

- use backchannel support when listening or use positive minimal responses: nodding, saying 'yeah' and 'mm hmm';
- hedge: use phrases, such as 'sort of', 'kind of', 'it seems like';
- use (super)polite forms: 'Would you mind ...', 'I'd appreciate it if ...', '... if you don't mind';
- use tag questions: 'You're going to dinner, aren't you?';
- use unhelpful adjectives: such as 'lovely', 'adorable', 'nice' and so on;
- use hypercorrect grammar and pronunciation;
- use direct quotation when quoting speech: 'She said, "You can't go."';
- have a special lexicon: use more words for things such as colours (like mauve or fuchsia);
- use question intonation in declarative statements: they make declarative statements into questions by raising the pitch of their voice at the end of a statement, expressing uncertainty;
- speak less frequently than men in public settings;

- apologize more often than men: 'I'm sorry, but I think that ...';
- use modal constructions: 'can', 'would', 'should', 'ought' – 'Should we turn up the heat?';
- avoid coarse language or expletives;
- use indirect commands and requests: for example, 'My, isn't it cold in here?' – as a request to turn the heat on or close a window;
- use more intensifiers than men, especially 'so' and 'very': for example, 'I am so glad you came!';
- lack a sense of humour: women do not tell jokes well and often don't understand the punch line of jokes;
- interrupt less often than men.

(Adapted from Lakoff, 1975).

Lakoff claimed that these linguistic features were typical of women's speech and, more importantly, that they indicated insecurity on the part of many women. She said:

Women's speech seems in general to contain more instances of 'well', 'you know', 'kind', and so forth: words that convey the sense that the speaker is uncertain about what [she] is saying. (p. 53)

Lakoff believed that women qualified their statements in such ways both because of their uncertainty and in order to subordinate themselves to others. Others disagreed. Lakoff's ideas sparked many possible interpretations of women's language patterns or tendencies. For one, non-verbal cues (such as eye-contact or touching or smiling) were said to also reflect power relations so that a focus only on spoken language was inadequate for the purposes of communication. Dale Spender (1980) had more to say about power in relationships and criticized Lakoff's view of women as deficient. She suggested that it had been men who dominated women as part of a patriarchal system so that women were not deficient as much as they were dominated. She also questioned the role of women themselves in creating their own domination. Perhaps if women spoke with more assertiveness they would be less dominated.

Pamela Fishman (1980) agreed with both Lakoff and Spender. Her research of conversations among heterosexual couples in romantic relationships suggested that, yes, women may ask more questions, use more backchannel support, and do most of the conversational work (what she called 'conversational shitwork'), and she saw these tendencies as being solely due to women's inferior position in society rather than any innate inabilities with language or socialized pattern. In fact, many women in Fishman's study were well able to cope with and through language, but they made specific linguistic choices that simply reflected a lack of power and even their own desire to remain in a powerless position in order to be in relationships with men. This, paradoxically, is also a form of power. That women may willingly collude in the power discrepancy is an important possibility. Fishman also suggested that conversations between the sexes sometimes fail, not because of anything inherent in the way women or men talk, but because of how men hold on to their role of centrality. Men do not need to provide much attentiveness in their conversations with women because they have markers of success outside these relationships that they find more meaningful to them, such as status and money.

Focusing on certain sex-preferential language tendencies, such as overlapping speech or questions or silence, reflects the participants' gendered patterns of interaction, but there remain various possibilities as to the intention or deliberate choice of certain speech behaviors. If a woman asks her silent male partner about his day, there are various elements at work to help understand his seeming lack of interaction. One can view a woman as weak in various conversations, as articulated in the deficit/dominance model, or one could view her as more engaged in conversations because she is a woman and is more prepared to ask questions and connect with others. This perspective is known as the difference model.

The differences perspective

Much work on men, women and language has looked for and at **sex differences**. In the 1970s, the sex differences found in language use were grouped together as 'sex-exclusive language styles', understood as women's or men's particular style of speaking. Later, 'sex-preferential speaking styles' where women and men had access to the same lexis, syntax and phonology, but they preferred to use some forms rather than others. This became a more popular way of labeling gendered language differences because this term could identify gendered styles with broad strokes of generalization. Now, gendered styles of language use are more often identified as tendencies.

Many, such as Deborah Tannen (1991, 1995, 1998), find the use of the term 'speech style' more helpful than the terms 'women's language' or 'men's language'. According to Tannen, very young children participate in gender-specific subcultures with distinct gender styles: the socialization process begins very early. Consequently, the words 'women' and 'men' are not particularly helpful in identifying gendered language patterns because children are also gendered in their language use from an early age. There are pressures on girls to 'be nice' and on boys to be competitive. It is difficult to know how such attitudes get transferred from one generation to another. It is likely that the attitudes connect with different interaction styles and personalities and linguistic choices made by individuals in particular groups and in particular settings. Maltz and Borker (1998) see that some of these linguistic choices work to disadvantage girls in certain ways and to disadvantage boys in other ways, but some do not. Girls seem to be more rehearsed into being collaborative in their use of language through playing with dolls and in paired groupings, while boys are often rehearsed into being more individual through sports. But both styles are useful and necessary. Girls (and women) may habitually use a conversational style of solidarity and come to thrive on it, while boys (and men) may opt for and develop styles based on competitiveness. But, either way, we have no clear idea as to whether or why this might be true in every case. Both styles of speaking can be beneficial to both groups, as well as detrimental in certain circumstances. The patterns and tendencies are infinitely complex and fluid so that generalizations are ultimately unhelpful.

Deborah Tannen (1991, 1995, 1998) has suggested that women's language style is largely based on the rehearsed role of many women to build relationships through language, while men are set up to monologue: rapport vs report. Tannen suggests that men and women speak in particular ways because they have been formed by the gender cultures into specific conversational roles and are thus most comfortable in them. She sets up masculine and feminine language as a series of contrasts: status vs support; independence vs intimacy; advice vs understanding; information vs feeling; orders vs proposals; conflict vs compromise. According to Tannen, both men and women are more comfortable with these highly gendered roles and continue to use their speech to support these gender roles.

Deborah Cameron (1995) has suggested that women have various and complex intentions for using any hesitant or passive forms of speech while Jennifer Coates (1993, 1996) has suggested that there is a function at work in the use of certain language techniques, namely to include the other speaker and to keep the conversation alive – something not necessarily associated with insecurity but rather with intelligence and even wisdom.

Most linguists exploring gender and language today would tend to agree that things said in any conversation depend on many variables, including the participant's age, experience, ethnic background, personality or temperament, as well as the context itself. Janet Holmes' (2003, 2006) work on women and men in the workplace strongly links intention to language use: what is intended influences both what is said and how it is understood. Her work also regards politeness as being aligned with gender – women being more polite than men, more often. Perhaps politeness is also aligned with life experiences and the perception of social rewards for politeness rather than with gender *per se*. Janet Holmes as well as Sara Mills (2003a) suggest that the ingredient of power is at the center of our relationships and, therefore, understanding power is most necessary in understanding language patterns and tendencies.

Other scholars, such as Victoria Bergvall (1999), have wondered if these discussions on masculine and feminine tendencies are at all helpful, because the focus itself on gender differences may support the view that such differences exist. That is, the exploration presupposes that women and men do speak differently, inviting essentialist explanations rather than the more helpful but also more complex social constructionist view. Why explore gender differences if we believe they are fluid and highly idiosyncratic? Perhaps, ultimately, the field of gender and language will become an historical one only, but this would seem to be a long way off.

Gendered identities and the social constructionist perspective

The social constructionist view is concerned with the specific social roles and positions we hold through language. In this view, we are each a 'constellation of subject positions bestowed by different discourses' (Talbot, 1998: 156). **Difference theory** argues that people are primarily defined by their gender as males and females, while social constructionism appreciates that there are a range of cultural and power factors at work which both reinforce and undermine our gender identities. Our subject positions develop in the activities within the particular institutions where we participate. For example, by going through a specific training experience one can become a language teacher, as I have done. This position of teacher is an effect of several education discourses. I have been given the words to use to contribute to this community in understood ways. Others in my field speak this same language: we use the same key vocabulary, share our understandings and define the boundaries of our group by speaking in understood ways to each other; we are specialists, as made evident in the way we speak. Our **subjectivity** reflects this. Any single individual is placed in a wide range of positions in various circumstances; this placement is known as subject positions or subjectivity. These positions are set up in a discourse, so much so that we cannot exist independently of discourse because we are constituted in the act of working within various discourses.

Subject positions shift throughout our lives. Even within the course of one day, one's subjectivity shifts many times; it is not fixed or even all that coherent. Our subjectivities are diverse and possibly even contradictory, displaying our remarkable ability to adapt and adjust our language use as necessary. Sometimes we play the role of expert on a topic; sometimes we are novices. Sometimes I am the expert teacher; sometimes I am new to a topic. Sometimes I am the hurt one in a relationship, and sometimes I am the one who hurts another. These shifts in subjectivity often produce tensions. Our sense of self is primarily constituted within relationships and within discourse so that self-determination itself can be hard to hold. I am who you see me to be and, likewise, you are who I see you to be. Our subject positions frame us.

Likewise, we perform our gendered identities because of the ways we've been rehearsed into specific discourses. For example, consider the over-used example of a young woman who affects crying when pulled over by police for speeding. The consequence of this gendered performance may result in a lenient penalty for her. The same consequence is unlikely if a young man performed in a similar way. Why? Because our interactions with the world are influenced by the ways we are understood by it and the ways we have been rewarded by certain behaviors by those around us. If we think of gender as performance, it can keep us from thinking people are passive participants in their own lives or that gender is a fixed category that traps us: it can also be used to liberate us. But while an actor is conscious of the role and behaves accordingly to achieve the best result possible in a given situation, we are often not conscious of the gender roles we play because we are so used to them: they feel 'natural'.

Social constructionism is also concerned with the way our social positions are fluid, negotiable and constantly changing, constantly renegotiated through linguistic and other types of performance. The repeated rehearsal of certain ways of speaking produce gender-differentiated performances. But these stylized gender positions are never absolutely fixed and we can choose our ways to participate in them. According to social constructionist theory, these positions are challenged and counteracted by the alternative ways in which people are positioned by power relations within a society, according to their age, class, ethnicity, education and sexuality (among other social variables). People have the potential to enact multiple identities. However, social constructionism also recognizes that certain dominant discourses in society (such as gender differentiation) have the power to produce particular identities longer term, which are harder to challenge or resist because of entrenched cultural approval for them.

Women and men talking

According to Mark Peters (2007) there is a persistent and stubborn myth (a dominant discourse) that women use more words per day than men. Peters indicates that women use about 7000 words a day compared to only 2000 for men. However, Peters uses the critiques voiced by Deborah Cameron that point to sexism as behind our willingness to believe that women talk more than men. '[The discrepancy] is hardly surprising', says Cameron, 'as the main influences on how much people speak are contextual – what they're doing and with whom' (in Peters, 2007: 21). The popular psychology industry seems to pander to such stereotypes in order to sell books when, in fact, no scholarly study has measured women speaking more than men.

Linguist Ann Bodine (1975) became popular for her identification of sex-preferential speech; she also suggested that sex-based tendencies were not absolute but, rather, were matters of degree. Years later, Deborah Tannen (1991) also used sex-preferential speech theory in her understanding of women and men as experiencing different gender cultures – something she saw as related to gendered communication cultures. Her colleague, John Gray (1994), wrote the best-selling book, *Men are from Mars, Women are from Venus*, which aligns sex-preferential speech styles with an essentialist understanding: 'women are like that' (meaning women are more collaborative in their communication tendencies) and 'men are like this' (meaning men are more competitive in their communication tendencies). Both Tannen and Gray remain popular figures with regards to explorations and explanations of communication difficulties between the sexes. Perhaps their popularity is due to their ability to simplify and align gender with sex-based characteristics. The 'different planets' idea is not ultimately very satisfying, however, because individuals can use dramatically different speech styles in different circumstances, with different participants and with different intentions.

Language use by anyone at all always depends on where it occurs, why, when, how and with whom. One person's language use will vary widely according to the needs of the social context, for instance in terms of the level of formality required and what is being discussed, and in regards to the relationship between and history of both speaker and listener(s). For example, the language I might use in a job interview or at an academic conference is very different from the language I use with my friends when discussing a film over a drink late on a Saturday night. In view of this, notions of sex-preferential speech patterns are helpful only to a point; none of us are simply a product of gender tendencies. We are all more than merely our gender.

Sex-preferential differences in language use are also highly culture-specific. Acquiring them is an important part of learning how to behave as men and women in a particular culture at a particular point in time. All speakers experience sex-preferential tendencies. What is convincing to me is the likelihood that we are both biologically rooted as well as socially interactive. We are many different versions of ourselves, in many different contexts and with various and altering intentions. Suffice it to say, our use of language reflects our human complexity and our ability to adapt to various situations.

Critical Discourse Analysis: the masculine as normative

What may appear natural or perhaps even 'normal' in our everyday lives as women or men is often a result of culturally produced roles that can become comfortable and connecting over time in our culture, though not always. These positions or identities can be entrapping and disempowering. But how does social construction happen? The gender difference becomes **normative** so that we think that what is feminine is something conciliatory, collaborative and person/relationship-oriented, while what is masculine is something more aggressive, competitive and task-oriented. These are broad statements to make a foundational point in understanding gender and language use: our genderedness may be arbitrary but it is reinforced through our life experiences and our interactions with each other.

In any community, there are various frames that restrict the conversations and define the reality of things. These ways of framing meaning and creating themes is what we call a 'discourse'. To explore the social construction of gender roles in language use, one of the main approaches used is known as **Critical Discourse Analysis (CDA)**. CDA is a perspective of language that is used within conversations and in social interactions. CDA is used to examine the way language contributes to both social reproduction and social change. The aim of CDA as a method of analyzing conversations is to stimulate and use a critical awareness of language to examine how a particular conversation emerges as a result of power relations between the participants. CDA is particularly helpful in gender and language studies because of its concern with power. Looking at language in this way can denaturalize it and allow the scholar some necessary objectivity. Sara Mills (1995) sees CDA as a way of asking questions about our notions of gender to 'create a productive suspicion of all processes of text interpretation' (p. 21).

CDA is one approach by which researchers in the field of gender and language consider how the masculine is constructed and how the feminine is constructed. Using CDA allows for consideration into how language is used for certain effect by participants. CDA can explore genderedness through language patterns and tendencies. Also, there are many possible discourses existing at any one time. Consider a conversation among extended family members at a family gathering. The discourses may include a discourse of success ('John has had a promotion at work') or a discourse of failure ('Mark has never got over his first marriage').

The French philosopher and social theorist, Michel Foucault (1972), considered discourse as both possibility and constraint and even predetermined within certain power relationships. For example, those in the legal profession use a body of knowledge, certain practices and social identities in their discourse. Legal discourse defines what is legal and illegal; these views are historically constituted and reinforced by the day-to-day use of certain words, terms and phrases associated with discussions concerning legal issues. Specific discourses determine what is understood and what is understandable. Foucault believed that knowledge itself does not necessarily reflect any particular truth, but rather it is discourse that reflects who has power and, therefore, knowledge. Foucault's view is that those who are dominant in any institution or group or community maintain their power and position through the use of specific discourse(s); they establish the boundaries of knowledge and they do this primarily through language use. For Foucault, power is what is exercised through discourse patterns. Foucault also investigated how knowledge defines identities through particular historical experiences of the Church and state – institutions that define our notions of deviance. Counterdiscourses propose alternative versions of social reality and, to Foucault, such counterdiscourses become important locations for the development of truth itself – if, in fact, any truth could ever be established.

If some people tend to use certain linguistic strategies (such as tag questions or hedges) more often than others, does this tendency suggest powerlessness? Surely different situations make different demands on different speakers. Some men (such as gay men, academic men, upper-class men, young metrosexuals) also use what Lakoff identified as women's language, suggesting perhaps that it is a certain type of person rather than men *per se* who might use more stereotypical male bravado language style (such as talking through interruptions, taking more linguistic space, or asking fewer questions to other participants). A more relational speech style might not be 'women's language' at all. What Lakoff posited in 1975 largely reflected her particular feminist political agenda that was relevant at the time, but it is no longer adequate for considering the variations of speech communities.

Although CDA attempts to deal with the complexity of subject positions and power relations, it tends to take a rather binary position where the males are the oppressors and the females are the oppressed. Judith Baxter (2003) articulates an alternative method: Feminist Post-structuralist Discourse Analysis (FPDA). Her approach challenges the traditional feminist view that females are often disempowered within mixed-sex settings. With an FPDA way of analyzing speech, one can consider that power relations are constructed in infinitely complex ways and that women are conscious beings who choose to participate in particular ways.

This chapter has briefly explored the relationship of gender and language use, particularly in relation to gender as a performance. The next few chapters look at some specific aspects of gender in context. Though there are numerous contexts where one could investigate the relationship of language and gender, the particular focus on media, on education, on the workplace, on the Christian Church, and on personal relationships opens up the awareness and the effect of this awareness in applied situations.

Summary statements	
	• Language use both reflects society's attitudes concerning men and women and constructs our attitudes toward and understandings of gender roles and expectations.
	• Various views of gendered language include the theory of deficit and/or dominance, the theory of difference and social constructionism; all views have been located at particular times and all have had some lasting influence.
	• CDA is now a common method used to explore gendered language patterns because it is concerned with power relations.

With a partner or on your own, consider:

1. How did Robin Lakoff's ideas from the mid-1970s influence the field of gender and language use? Why was her description of 'women's language' problematic then and why is it now?

2. If searching for gender differences presupposes that there are differences, what else can be said about the relationship of gender and language use? Why study the relationship at all? What use is it?

3. How and why does CDA serve as an important method of interpretation? Explain how FPDA offers an alternative way of analyzing speech.

Further reading

To read more on the study of gender and language use using either the perspective of deficit/dominance theory or difference theory, consider:

Cameron, D. (2007) *The Myth of Mars and Venus: Do Men and Women Really Speak Different Languages?* Oxford: Oxford University Press.

Coates, J. (2004) *Women, Men and Language* (3rd edn). New York: Pearson.

Gray, J. (1994) *Men are from Mars, Women are from Venus: A Practical Guide for Improving Communication and Getting What You Want.* New York: Harper Collins.

Lakoff, R. (1975) *Language and Woman's Place.* New York: Harper and Row.

Spender, D. (1980) *Man Made Language.* London: Pandora.

Tannen, D. (1991) *You Just Don't Understand: Women and Men in Conversation.* New York: William Morrow.

Also, I recommend these books on the use of CDA and its FPDA alternative:

Baxter, J. (2003) *Positioning Gender in Discourse: A Feminist Methodology.* Basingstoke: Palgrave.

Lazar, M. (ed.) (2005) *Feminist Critical Discourse Analysis: Studies in Gender, Power and Ideology.* London: Palgrave Macmillan.

Part 2:
Understanding gender and language use in various contexts

3

Gender and language use in the media

This chapter explores language use within media and investigates how language is used to create compelling advertising as well as a tool to advance particular ways of being male and female by asking these questions:

- How do the mass media use gender to produce consumers for specific products – and why is the use of gender so effective as a tool for advertising?

- What is 'raunch culture' and how is gender used to exploit the desires of young people?

- Why do role models in the media have such influence on both boys and girls? Does it matter to us how femininity and masculinity are presented in film, TV and advertising?

- What is 'consumer gender'?

- Why is the presentation of an impossible gendered 'ideal' (the 'ideal' woman, the 'ideal' man) so compelling?

'Advertisers in general bear a large part of the responsibility for the deep feelings of inadequacy that drive [us] to psychiatrists, pills, or the bottle.'
Marya Mannes (*But Will It Sell?*, 1964)

It is easy to see that gender in capitalist societies aligns with sexualization: hyper masculine and feminine images sell. Conventional kinds of feminine and masculine appearance are shaped by the mass media to produce consumers for specific products. Being feminine and masculine involves particular modes of behavior and consumption; advertising creates in us all a need for a gendered identity because gender is singled out as what needs to be worked on, enhanced and supplied. When we go shopping, we make decisions to genderize ourselves using the products marketed to us. Many media themes and images reflect the power relations in society and use our aspirations to attract us to particular products. Clothing and cosmetic companies in particular depend on gendered identities to sell their products. This chapter introduces you to gender as an advertising agent as well as to media discourse and its complex connection with gender construction and gender maintenance.

Gender identity and the mass media

David Gauntlett (2002) identifies a number of themes connecting gender identity and the media, including the fluidity of our gender identities over time, the decline of the portrayal of traditional gender roles, the idea of gender role models and the rise of a new 'girl power'. Twenty or 30 years ago, analysis of popular media often told researchers that mainstream culture was a backwards-looking force, resistant to social change and able to push people into traditional categories they might be trying to leave behind. Today, researchers are more likely to view mass media as a force for change. The traditional view of a woman as housewife has been replaced by successful and raunchy 'girl power' icons, and the masculine ideals of toughness and self-reliance have been shaken by a new emphasis on men's emotions. These alternative ideas and images have created a space for a diversity of identities but they also bring with them new demands and requirements.

Ariel Levy (2005) identified the 'raunch' culture and its grip on today's young women. She explores the internalizing of misogyny by women who not only participate in this culture but also encourage their own exploitation. Mary Pipher (1994) identified in the 1990s how adolescent girls internalize society's messages about appearance and thinness in particular. She comes down hardest on advertisers who push the image of attractive women to impossible standards, profiling isolated body parts (backside, legs, cleavage) to sell perfection. This focus on isolated sections removes any chance to personalize the female form and leads young women to believe that they are only valuable if their body parts look a particular way.

However, David Gauntlett (2002) sees gender role models in the media as cultural 'navigation points' for individual members of society. For him, the discourses of 'girl power' concerning sexuality and gender roles are today's most prominent expressions of <u>femininity</u> in the mainstream media and can be empowering to many young women. The media disseminates a huge number of messages about identity and acceptable forms of self-expression, gender, sexuality and lifestyle. At the same time, we have our own set of diverse feelings on these issues, which can change as we move through different life stages. The media's suggestions are seductive, but can never simply overpower contrary feelings in the audience. If the media is sexist, the culture is as well. Even if we agree that many media sources sustain traditional hierarchical notions of femininity and benefit from it, we can't ignore the participation and choice that women themselves make: they like the products and choose to buy them (Caldas-Coulthand, 1996). Women seek out women's magazines and want the practical tips in them. Consequently, we can expect that the specific messages will be appropriated by many even if rejected by some readers or viewers.

The *See Jane* organization, a media-watch program, was founded by Oscar award winning actress Geena Davis in 2004. Its research is carried out by Stacy Smith (2006a, 2006b) at the University of Southern California, Los Angeles, and explores G-rated (G for General – family viewing) movies and the portrayal of female and male characters in films marketed to children. Smith and her team explored 101 top-grossing family-rated films released from 1990 through to 2004, analyzing a total of 4249 speaking characters in the movies, including both animated and live action films. The research found that, overall, three out of four characters (75%) are male, while fewer than one in three (28%) speaking characters are female. Fewer than one in five (17%) characters in crowd scenes are female and more than four out of five (83%) film narrators are male. Smith (2006b) also found that G-rated movies show very few examples of characters as parents or as partners in a marriage or other committed relationship.

For all of us, but especially for children, images and stories help influence the important developmental task of understanding what it means to be human, whether male or female. In a 2003 American nationwide survey, the Kaiser

Family Foundation found that half of all children aged zero to six watch at least one DVD movie per day. In view of this, G-rated movie DVDs may have an influence on children's early social learning about gender roles because children also tend to watch the same movie over and over. Other studies explore the television viewing habits among children and suggest that gender expectations can become very simplified, skewed and stereotypical in nature (Herrett-Skjellum & Allen, 1996). Since women and girls make up half of the human race, the *See Jane* media watch group in particular believes the presence of a wider variety of female characters in children's earliest experiences with the media is essential for both girls' and boys' development. If both boys and girls see more female characters of all types, we can experience a fuller awareness of the possible ways to be human.

In 2002, the director-actor Rosanna Arquette made a documentary film called *Searching for Debra Winger* about how hard it is to be a female actor in Hollywood. She wanted to answer the question: Can a woman have both her art and a life? She interviewed a wide range of very successful Hollywood women, including Jane Fonda, Meg Ryan, Sharon Stone and Vanessa Redgrave. Eventually, Arquette's search leads her to the home of Debra Winger herself, an Oscar award winning actor who stopped making films. Winger offers few insights, saying that she never really liked acting anyway and that is the reason she quietly retired from her Hollywood life. However, the other actors interviewed along the way say much more about how difficult, even impossible, it is to have both an acting career and a personal life as a woman: the demands on both personal time and appearance are unrelenting. All mention the lack of roles available for women over 40 in particular and the use for younger women in a narrow variety of roles within a very narrow definition of attractiveness: young, skinny, long hair, clear skin, perfect teeth. The demands are exhausting. If women in Hollywood resist it, the industry can find many others who will fit the **ideal**. In this way, expertise and talent that grow with age are not rewarded as are youth and rare beauty.

Advertising gender

The media images of female beauty are unattainable for most women. Jean Kilbourne (2000) reports that women's magazines have ten and a half times more advertisements and articles promoting weight loss than do men's magazines, and over 75% of women's magazines' covers include at least one message about how to change a woman's bodily appearance. Twenty years ago, the average model weighed 8% less than the average women, but today's models weigh 23% less. The barrage of messages about thinness, dieting and beauty tells ordinary women that they are always in need of adjustment and women internalize these stereotypes and judge themselves harshly (Kilbourne, 2000).

Jean Kilbourne's work points out the dreamlike promise of advertising that leaves us never satisfied: we can always improve something. The barrage of advertising (some 3000 advertisements produced per day) affects young people in particular, creating an 'addictive mentality' that often continues throughout life. Why are standards of beauty being imposed on women, the majority of whom are naturally larger and older than any of the models? Because by presenting an ideal difficult to achieve and maintain, the cosmetic and diet industries are assured of growth and profits. Women who are insecure about their bodies are more likely to buy beauty products, new clothes and diet aids. Exposure to images of thin, young, air-brushed female bodies is linked to depression and loss of self-esteem and the need to do whatever is necessary to conform to acceptability.

In modern industrial societies, gender identities are heavily determined and influenced by the capitalist interests that propel the market. In their roles as wives and mothers, women are often the ones responsible for most of the shopping. As a result, women are often caught up in what is called **consumer femininity** – women buy certain products and buy into the need for them in order to feminize themselves. Consumerism also affects men, promoting **consumer masculinity** – buying things specifically to enhance a masculine image. **Consumer gender** enters our daily relationships, how we view ourselves, and is a major influence on our patterns at work, in the home and in our friendships and relationships with others. Consumer gender is largely a construction of the mass media in which we co-participate. We spend our time and money to construct ourselves as acceptable versions of ourselves, which requires much effort and, more importantly, much expense.

The construction of gender identities in advertising is both fascinating and disturbing. The process is highly manipulative. The types of femininities and masculinities are established and reinforced through the existence of and insistence on an assumed audience. While the media producers construct an ideal, we, the consumers, position ourselves in relation to that ideal (Fairclough, 1989, 1992, 1995). Distancing oneself from the ideal involves some awareness of it. As viewers or readers, we are assumed to be 'normal' and the market establishes a 'consensus' of which we join (Hall *et al.*, 1978). This is particularly visible in women's magazines and the creation of femininity and definitions of what is both 'normal' and normative. By and large, media is propelled by the market (us) and our views and values; the media can't create what's not already there, but it can create more exaggerated forms. Advertising expands on our deep human values and desires to create an even greater need for certain products.

Media discourse

Though there are magazines and television programming targeted at men and demanding of them in similar ways, the range of media targeted at women is staggering: fashion magazines, women's home-making magazines, celebrity magazines, women's television networks, daytime talk shows, daytime soap-operas, food channels. Lia Litosseliti (2006: 97) lists several UK women's magazines each connecting with their ideal audience. In each case, the magazine uses phrases to brand itself as connected to its audience. Consider the use of language as found on the covers of these magazines:

- *Cosmopolitan*: The world's no. 1 magazine for young women
- *She*: For women who know what they want
- *B*: Everything you want
- *Woman's Own*: For the way you live your life and the way you'd like to
- *Company*: For your freedom years
- *Minx*: For girls with a lust for life
- *Executive woman*: For women who really do mean business
- *Wench*: Where women are, where they are going, and where they should be already.

Litosseliti highlights the use of personal pronouns ('you', 'your', 'we') as a common feature which assumes and thereby creates a relationship between the publisher and the consumer. As a result, there is a fabrication and creation of an agreed ideal. The use of personal phrases in editorials (such as 'most of us' or 'we've all done it') makes manipulated connections with a reader that creates a solidarity or, as Mary Talbot (1995) called this solidarity, a **synthetic sisterhood**. This artificial construction of a feminine-gender community is located in an ideal setting where economic or social differences are not made explicit. As a result, any woman can imagine herself as part of the sisterhood promoted. What seems to matter is that consumers feel a kindred connection and, hence, there is an establishment of a loyal consumer relationship. Men's products work in a similar way: a community is assumed, then created and then a relationship emerges with certain key products that enhance the gender identity of its consumers. Any glance at a magazine stand will demonstrate the use of ideal images to sell a need to improve oneself.

Talbot (1995) is critical of the creation of a consumer femininity in particular because of the representation of women as helpless, gullible consumers. In order to belong, women must look a certain way (new each season) and share common values and tastes to be fully acceptable. Hence, women are rehearsed into a powerless femininity for the sake of a consumer-driven market. They seek out participation and belonging but then are trapped. By comparison, men are usually shown images of men in positions of power, freedom and independence, so that women are the ones who lose the most from media's portrayal of them. The demands on men may be as demanding as those placed on women, but their hypothetical rewards are more empowering. They 'get to be' rich and powerful, while all that women can hope for is to be physically appealing and, hopefully, thin. Although most contemporary research on masculinity in the media has focused on violence in TV and film, some research has begun to examine the portrayal of masculinity in men's magazines such as *Maxim*, *GQ* and *Esquire*. These magazines also play a part in defining what it means to be a modern man through the same use of a synthetic community.

Most of our popular magazines, television shows and movies assume a heterosexual audience and reinforce the presupposition that women and men are biologically very different and, as a direct result, are quite distinct and not that complex or ambiguous. Men and women, boys and girls, are polarized in the media in terms of values, behaviors and styles. This in turn influences our views of gender differences: we come to see the stereotypical portrayal of gender as normal. We see the Old Spice (American cologne) man as 'naturally' masculine, rather than manipulated for the sake of the sale. Even newer images have created a version of masculinity that is narrow, though now also concerned with relationships, fashion, health, fitness and appearance. This 'new man' is in some ways a positive development, but it is also a confusing one. On the one hand, he is aligned with traditional masculinity based on male success, wealth, power and heterosexual desire; on the other hand, however, he must also be connected to his friends and his family. There is a conflict here of traditional and progressive discourses of masculinity, such as the conflicts in the representations of women.

Some see the various discourses used in advertising suggest that the language of advertising more often places women in the personal consumer position (the shopper) while treating men as autonomous and independent selves. For example, 'Ladies, look for ...' while 'Men, insist on ...' (see Myers, 1994, 1998). Most advertisements are targeted to a specific gendered consumer and we are 'spoken' to in particularly gendered ways. The images in magazines and in advertisements elsewhere create a fantasy world where identity is achieved through clothes, make-up, social setting – in short, through the use of a gender-targeted product. The phrasing used to sell products connects with our gendered worlds.

All gender polarization works on a level of assumption or presupposition about desire and desirability – that men desire attractive women and that women want men's attention and approval or men are portrayed as victims of feminism, highlighting the new dilemma regarding how to be a man. Thus, the earlier feminist discourses of deficit/dominance are appropriated for the promotion of the male experience – the argument apparently being that men are now used for woman's purposes (such as to help around the house or to supply them with money, travel and so on). Michelle Lazar (2005) refers to this trend as a discourse of 'popular post-feminism' or a 'global neo-liberal discourse of post-feminism', which states that, now that certain gains for women have been made, feminism has achieved its purpose and should therefore be dropped: the victim is now male. However, these constructions of alleged equality between the sexes, or even a reversal of gender roles and power, obscure the actual gender inequalities that persist in women's and men's real life experiences. Even with counter-images, our gender is used to create and sell illusions of identity.

It is doubtful that news producers and journalists are immune to all distorted gender representations. Sara Mills (2003b) examines how the news media texts are authored and how different criteria influences what is reported, how and by whom (a woman or a man). Both talk shows and news broadcasts are fascinating sites for gender studies. Mills describes a variety of factors for the selection of primary news items, arguing that male television anchors are seen as more authoritative while women more often present 'soft' human interest stories, rather than 'hard' news. Media and cultural studies analyses since the 1980s have turned attention to how audiences use texts using CDA to identify processes of gender creation. Successful television programming, for example, connects with specific target audiences – audiences which align with particular attitudes and life experiences. These target audiences are often gender based. Take, for example, the popular *Oprah Winfrey Show*, watched by over six million viewers a day. This talk show connects with middle-class women who are concerned about their families, their relationships with spouses and friends, their appearance and their home decorating – all stereotypical concerns of women. Do such shows reveal attitudes already 'out there' or do they promote a particular range of concerns directed at a market niche? It is likely to be both.

It is fascinating but also problematic to consider the ways in which gender is used and promoted in the media. The media serves as both a mirror and a tool of gender stereotyping. It is therefore worth considering its power to coerce and manipulate. Gender images are used to advertise certain products. If a need or desire can be developed, then a product can be marketed to fill the need. If my gray hair is seen as undesirable for women my age, then I will buy the necessary product(s) to correct this deficiency. It is the promotion of an ideal (done through images as well as through language) that creates the need. It is the specific use of created gender ideals in both image and in discourse that make the study of gender and language in the media particularly fascinating. However, a post-structuralist perspective would argue that individuals are not trapped by such positionings and can negotiate new positions and roles. Through questioning, challenging and over-turning, we can and do construct ever-new ways to be in the world.

Summary statements

- Conventional kinds of feminine and masculine appearance are shaped by the mass media to produce consumers for various products. Consumer gender is intricately connected to our gendered identities.
- We participate in consumer femininity and consumer masculinity in order to genderize ourselves; this participation influences our daily relationships and is a major part of our patterns of behavior at work, at home and in our friendship groups.
- Though men can be objectified in media images, the manipulation of women seems to be more prevalent and more destructive because media images often present women as objects of male desire or even promoting a cultural misogyny that is embedded in her helplessness or, if not beautiful, her invisibility.

With a partner or on your own, consider:

1. Think of two or three different kinds of TV programs and consider the advertisements used to support each one. What do the advertisements suggest about the assumed audience in each case? How is gender used by advertisers to create a need?

2. Explain the terms consumer gender and synthetic sisterhood. How do both women and men genderize themselves based on the products marketed to them? Why do feminists think that using gender in the media is problematic?

3. Why is gender used by the media in such stereotypical ways? Why is it so effective, even as gender roles adjust and change, to use gender identity as a location of needs and desires?

Further reading

To read more on the use of gender and language in the media, see:

Caldas-Coulthard, C. (1995) Man in the news: The misrepresentation of women in the news-as-narrative discourse. In S. Mills (ed.) *Language and Gender: Interdisciplinary Perspectives* (pp. 226–39). Harlow: Longman.

Cook, G. (2001) *The Discourse of Advertising* (2nd edn). London: Routledge.

Fairclough, N. (1995) *Media Discourse*. London: Arnold.

Gauntlett, D. (2002) *Media, Gender and Identity: An Introduction*. New York: Routledge.

Hermes, J. (1995) *Reading Women's Magazines*. Cambridge: Polity.

Koller, V. (2004) *Metaphor and Gender in Business Media Discourse: A Critical Cognitive Study*. Basingstoke: Palgrave.

Kilbourne, J. (2000) *Can't Buy My Love: How Advertising Changes the Way We Think and Feel*. Washington, DC: Free Press.

Mills, S. (1995) *Feminist Stylistics*. London: Routledge.

Myers, G. (1998) *Ad Worlds: Brands, Media, Audiences*. London: Arnold.

Wetherall, A. (2002) *Gender, Language and Discourse*. London: Psychology Press.

4

Gender and language use in education

This chapter explores the intersection of language use and education by asking these key questions:

- How do boys and girls experience education in similar ways? How do they experience education in gendered ways?

- At what age do we think gender identity becomes fixed?

- How is it that our gender identities change throughout our educational experiences?

- In what ways do teachers serve to rehearse students into gendered roles? How is language used as a major tool for the teacher as a gender coach?

- Why is the consideration of linguistic space used in classrooms helpful in an understanding of gender as performance? What does the silence tell us?

- How does language play a part in the underachievement of boys?

'The emotional, sexual, and psychological stereotyping of females begins when the doctor says, "It's a girl".'
Shirley Chisholm, American politician, educator and author (1924–2005)

The vast area of education is of concern to many of us, including the parents, the students themselves, the communities and people surrounding schools and the larger society more generally. All of these stakeholders understand, to some extent, that the relationship we have with our educational institutions connect us with certain life successes. In particular, classrooms and the surrounding school culture are important settings for the foundations of social behavior. The construction of one's gender identity and the resulting relationship with the world is rehearsed day in and day out inside schools. Thus, gender, language use and education are inevitably and intimately connected. This chapter explores the relationship of gender and schooling, gender and teacher behavior, as well as gender performances inside classrooms.

Gender and the school experience

There is a substantial and wide-ranging body of research connecting gender with achievement. Some studies have focused particularly on teacher–student interaction (see Jule, 2004; Mahony, 1985; Spender, 1982; Stanworth, 1983) while other studies have focused on student–student interactions (see Baxter, 2003; Swann & Graddol, 1995). More recent work marks a shift away from any gender generalizations or differences to examine the discourses and the various gender identities that are at work in various educational settings (see AAUWEF, 1992; Baxter, 1999; Pavlenko & Piller, 2001).

It is the specific structures surrounding classrooms and classroom life that are of particular interest in the study of gender and language use. Many researchers have offered various pieces to the puzzle. For example, Rebecca Oxford's (1994) work on gender differences in language classrooms focuses on learning styles noted in females and the particular learning strategies often employed by those born male. After some discussion of possible differences (such as subjectivity or objectivity, reflection or sensory preference among female learners) she concluded by saying gender has a strong connection to the educational experience. She said:

Anatomy is not destiny, as Freud suggested, but a learner's sex – or, more likely, gender – can have profound effects on the ways that learners approach language learning, ways which may in turn affect proficiency. (p. 146)

One of the themes running through the earlier work of Valerie Walkerdine (1990) is that all classrooms are 'sites' of some struggle and often sites of passive and silent struggles on the part of many girls, struggling against a host of gendered expectations. Struggles to participate may exist because of the power relations. The classrooms in Walkerdine's research revealed offensive and, at times, aggressive language use on the part of male students directed towards their female teachers and female classmates. Other studies, too, have found maleness to be a major indicator of power and legitimacy in schools, as demonstrated through certain gendered speech practices, both inside classrooms and on school playgrounds. Research that has focused on primary classrooms (such as nursery schools, reception classes, kindergartens) has explored language used in the very early years of schooling. Geoffrey Short and Bruce Carrington's (1990) research of young children's attitudes, for example, suggests the possibility that gender roles and expectations are prescribed early in life, are easily accepted by children and remain relatively stable; more specifically, they argue that children view gender as a fixed element of themselves and others by the age of five. When the children in their study were asked directly about gender roles, they responded with traditional gender stereotyping comments (such as, 'mommies cook', 'daddies build things'); and a significant number of children spoke of such traditional gender roles as 'natural' and as permanent characteristics.

Some roles or habits in classrooms seem to reflect the patriarchy of society in general, which sees more power being equated to the male or the masculine and less power as equated to the female or the feminine. A lack of self-esteem among many girls may be the main point of concern when considering gender in the classroom, particularly in secondary schooling (Pipher, 1994). Girls tend to describe themselves in fundamentally different ways to those used by their boy classmates. For example, girls' comments generally suggest that they perceive themselves to be less able, less capable and they construct themselves in more self-demeaning and modest ways than do boys in similar situations (Szirom, 1988). Research in this area suggests that both boys and girls participate in creating power differences and that they are most likely to do this as a way of belonging to their various classroom communities.

Observational studies have examined what children do in classrooms when selecting certain toys or books – girls select more stereotypical feminine items, such as dolls, and boys select more stereotypical masculine items, such as trucks and blocks. Such studies have also looked at which stories teachers read to children and how gender is presented in these stories – who is the main character? Who are the antagonists? These items often align with gender stereotypes. The earlier interactional analysis work of Nicholas Flanders (1970) found teacher-dominated approaches in most classrooms, approaches that limit student contributions in general and perhaps female contributions in particular, because student contributions rely on report-style discussions – something that seems to be more comfortable for boys to perform. This interpretation emerges from difference theory; understanding males and females through the lens of difference.

The teacher as gender coach

According to David Corson (1993), many studies have confirmed that teachers not only seem to be unaware that they treat boys and girls differently, but also even disbelieve the evidence when confronted with it. Indeed, it appears common for teachers to defend their actual practices with a sincere disclaimer that they 'treat them all the same' (p. 144).

Because classrooms are filled with language, students are engaged with language for most of the day. If there are consistently marked and consistent patterns in the ways boys and girls participate in their classrooms, what are these tendencies and what are the implications? Dale Spender and Elizabeth Sarah (1980) believed that girls were the ones who were

'learning how to lose' at the game of education, undemanding of teacher time, passive, background observers to boys' active learning ... and to strive for success within traditional, domestic, nurturing careers. (p. 27)

Also, regardless of test scores or academic achievement that has been most recently in favor of girls, girls' 'success' in education and throughout life remains a complex and contradictory issue. Higher test scores on the part of girls do not seem to serve as an indication of high success later in life (Davies, 2003). Even when girls do appear to 'win' at the education game, they lose out on long-term achievement.

Joanna Thornborrow's (2002) research highlights the ways in which teachers control classroom participation through their 'teacher talk'. She sees teacher talk as creating and maintaining asymmetrical power relationships. Teacher-led classroom talk as a pedagogical approach is often organized around initiation/response/follow-up exchanges in which the teacher controls the students by controlling the dynamics of classroom discourse: 'the teacher takes turns at will, allocates turns to others, determines topics, interrupts and reallocates turns judged to be irrelevant to these topics, and provides a running commentary on what is being said and meant' (p. 176).

Thornborrow's conclusions match up with earlier feminist ideas that point to classrooms as sites of patriarchy. Pat Mahony (1985), for example, understood teacher attention swayed towards boys to be an indication of prevailing societal attitudes that stem from attitudes at large: boys are privileged learners because males are privileged participants in society and this privilege is evident in the way boys monopolize teacher attention. In Mahony's study, for every two boys asking questions there was only one girl.

Michelle Stanworth's (1983) work also explored gender divisions in classroom talk, and her conclusions also pointed significantly to teacher control of classroom talk. She said:

The important point is not that girls are being 'discriminated against', in the sense of being graded more harshly or denied educational opportunities but that the classroom is a venue in which girls and boys, dependent upon a man (or woman) who has a considerable degree of power over their immediate comfort and long-term future, can hardly avoid becoming enmeshed in a process whereby 'normal' relationships between the sexes are being constantly defined. (p. 18)

Studies involving protracted observation of a variety of classrooms have shown, almost invariably, that boys receive a disproportionate share of teachers' time and attention. My own research has examined the use of gendered linguistic space in various classrooms, from primary to post-secondary. In each case, boys and young men spoke disproportionately more (see Jule, 2004, 2005, 2007). High achieving boys are a particularly favoured group, claiming more of their teachers' energies than both similarly performing girls and less successful pupils of either sex. On the other hand, although girls are criticized at least as often as boys for academic mistakes, boys are far more often reprimanded for misconduct and, in some classrooms, these criticisms account for a large share of the extra attention directed at boys.

It has been well argued by both Mahony and Stanworth, as well as many other educational researchers, that the implicit message to all students is that the extra time given to male students may suggest to both boys and girls that boys are simply more interesting to the teacher: '[B]y more frequently criticizing their male pupils, teachers may unwittingly reinforce the idea that the "naughtiness" of boys is more interesting, more deserving, than the "niceness" of girls' (Stanworth, 1983: 19).

In addition to the extra attention paid to boys and the more dynamic talk between teachers and boys, there is girls' relative silence. Spender (1980) examined the patterns of silence among female students and reflected on the 'chattering female' stereotype. That is, we perceive girls as chatty when in fact they are not very vocal at all in full classroom lessons. Spender said that both sexes bring to the classroom an understanding that it is the boys who should 'have the floor' and females who should be dutiful and attentive listeners. She believed that, within educational institutions, girls are made aware that their talk is evaluated differently from the boys, in view of which they generally shut up. However, it is important to recognize this research emerges from a dominance perspective: the females are being dominated by oppressive males.

Linguistic space and silence

Of particular concern to me is the unique connection of gender, speech and silence – and a concept Mahony (1985) first termed as the distribution of 'linguistic space' in the classroom. Mahony found that it was 'normal' for a teacher to ignore girls for long periods of time, for boys to call out and for boys to dominate classroom talk in addition to dominating the actual physical space. Some would say the teacher demands such active engagement of the boys. This evidence of gendered language tendencies regarding the use of linguistic space in classrooms may derive from both the particular features of the language used (particular patterns and habits of belonging) as well as the amount or proportion of talk-time in teacher-led lessons. People follow implicit rules in order to belong to their classroom community (Lave & Wenger, 1991). I found similar patterns in my own classrooms and in the classrooms I researched (Jule, 2004). But to make claims about both the quality of language as well as the quantity of words spoken reinforces gender divisions and, as such, verges on essentialism connecting with a difference perspective.

Karen Bailey (1993) also saw gender roles as constructed through language and that teachers, in particular, pass on a social order through their own use of speech, including the proportions of talk-time allocated to different classroom participants. Such 'gendering' may be seen most obviously in the proportion of talk-time. Even if or when the attention paid to boys is negative, their very presence in the classroom claims more teacher time and focus. This view is also expressed by Carrie Paechter (1998). She, too, views teachers' attempts to get boys to consent to their authority as one reason they allow boys more control over physical space, teacher attention and lesson content. But with the growth in emphasis on the importance of student-centered learning, classroom talk is increasingly seen as central to the learning process. A range of international research has persuasively demonstrated that the skill to speak effectively in public confers social and/or professional prestige and that this usually falls to the males in any given society (Baxter, 1999, 2003; Coates, 1993; Holmes, 1998; Jones & Mahony, 1989; Nichols, 1983; Tannen, 1995). Speaking up in class is not just important for the opportunity to engage with ideas or with language: it signifies and creates important social power and legitimacy.

Relationships within classrooms may well propel the gender imbalance seen in society more generally. A loss of opportunity to speak aloud may result in lower confidence and having less recognition or involvement when girls do participate. In the rapid exchange of classroom discussions involving teacher–student talk, it is often the first student to respond by raising a hand or making eye-contact with the teacher who receives the attention of the class. Swann (1992, 1998) and many others suggest that such quick responders are usually male. By engaging in a form of privileged interaction, teachers are not only distancing those who may be less competitive or aggressive, but also giving those who already excel in claiming the floor (often the boys) further opportunities to do so.

If girls and boys tend to have markedly different patterns in their use of language in many classrooms and across various age groups, then these patterns may reflect the language patterns around them, as well as develop these patterns further. If teaching methods offer little recognition of the possibility of gendered language experiences and create unequal language opportunities for the students as a result – in short, if there is a marked gender difference in the use of linguistic space – this needs to be further examined by researchers and classroom teachers alike.

In Lakoff's (1975) work, she called for a 'relearning of language' that would require those born female to recognize those speech patterns that undermine power, throw off their 'learned helplessness', and simply speak more like men. However, when applied to classroom life in particular, there is no empirical evidence to suggest that if girls used more interruptions, for example, that this would dismantle patriarchy and create greater female power. Day-to-day experiences are too complicated for simplistic self-help directives. Nevertheless, awareness of gendered tendencies in classroom talk is an important step in establishing some gender parity and understanding the gender divide in education. The particular feature of silence among so many girls and women is distinct from the identification and examination of other distinctive tendencies in female speech. Nancy Goldberger (1997: 254) reports that 'silence is an issue not just for a subset of women ... but is a common experience, albeit with a host of both positive and negative connotations'. Most researchers now agree that silence is a consistently observed feature of girls in many classrooms across all age groups, in various socio-economic groups, and in all subject areas. Mary Pipher's (1994) work explores the relationship between adolescent girls' developmental stage and their desire to be desired by boys: their silence is part of their feminine attractiveness. Talkative girls are viewed by boys as less desirable.

Both Robin Lakoff (1995) and Adam Jaworski (1993) admit that not all silence is necessarily about power and powerlessness, but both advise researchers to consider this possibility. There are particularly two of Lakoff's women's speech patterns that relate to silence: lack of interruption and lack of topic control (cf. West & Zimmerman, 1987). Lakoff suggests that if one is interrupted, then, in a sense, one is silenced by being stopped. It seems that girls will stop speaking when interrupted in part to align with the gender role of silence as befitting those born female: they are more acceptable when quiet. Susan Gal (1991) was clearer than Lakoff in asserting that there is a massive distinction between self-imposed silence and externally imposed silence, although this may be difficult to perceive from a research perspective. There is evidence to suggest that a sense of feeling silenced and of feeling unheard are painful and frustrating experiences to many (maybe most) girls in school. To be ignored when speaking (either intentionally or not) is the equivalent of being told that you know nothing or have nothing to say worth hearing. Lakoff (1995) believed that the situation of ignoring female speech in classroom situations, such as not offering eye-contact or a sound of recognition, is a particularly poignant way of silencing her because of the traditional and consistent power discrepancies that align with gender roles.

In the 1970s, Zimmerman and West (1975) reported that the length of silences by both male and female participants when in mixed-sex settings was three times as long as in single-sex settings. Minimal responses ('hmmm', 'uh huh') were offered by males in mixed-sex settings, but only after a considerable length of silence. Such a delay of even minimal response on the part of boys and men was thought to indicate a lack of significance to a female speaker. Both Zimmerman and West (1975) and later, Pamela Fishman (1983) pointed to the listener as an active participant of some sort, even when the listener was silent. But if the silent listener was male, his silence was interpreted by researchers as his lack of interest; while if a silent listener was female, it seemed to indicate her lack of significance. Conversational control was (and perhaps still is) often subtly achieved by a nonresponse, and nonresponse is not infrequent in classrooms: 'When a female student raises her hand and is recognized, her comment often receives no response' (Lakoff, 1995: 28). In my own research in primary classrooms, I too saw a pattern of female responses to teacher questions as limited in interaction, often a quick nod or affirmation. Boys, on the other hand, seemed to receive considerably more verbal interaction with the teacher when they ventured to respond (see Jule, 2004). However, silence may or may not be a conscious strategy on the part of females. Coates (1993) examines silence in her discussion of the societal perception of female 'verbosity' and our cultural requirement for females to say less. She cites studies that found men took longer to describe a picture (average 13 minutes) than women (average 3 minutes); and that males took up to four times the linguistic space in most conversations. Coates suggests that the myth of females as talkative leads to certain expectations concerning who has the right to talk in classrooms, too. She agrees here with Spender's (1980) hypothesis that female speech is often seen as empty chatter, while what men say is regarded as important and significant.

The classroom as gender stage

Most recent research explains the underachievement of boys as being in part due to a growing culture of masculinity that insists on a lack of interest in academic pursuits – 'lad culture', as it is commonly referred to in Britain (Altani, 1995; Baxter, 1999; Connell, 1995; Davies, 2003; Epstein *et al.*, 1998; Mac an Ghaill, 2000; Yates, 1997). Boys' growing lack of engagement with schooling has led to a 'moral panic' of sorts and a reactionary grappling for more classroom support for boys, rather than for girls. If the boys are not excelling, then our civilization is in grave danger! This issue is an explosive one in schooling systems around the world, with boys' underachievement as a growing focus of much recent feminist discussions (Baxter, 1999, 2003; Mac an Ghaill, 2000). The American Association of University Women Educational Foundation (AAUWEF, 1992) points out that 'one year out of college, women working full time earn only 80% as much as men earn' even with the same educational experiences. Men consistently choose careers that pay better and require more of them; women choose less demanding and less financially rewarding work. Regardless of success at school, boys achieve more – not less.

However, such discussions seem to be settling on any 'underachievement' of boys as unlikely to benefit girls in the long run because 'discursive practices continue to constitute girls' school successes in limited and derogatory ways' (Baxter, 1999: 94). Judith Baxter believes that even if and when girls 'win' they still 'lose', 'winning' at tests but 'losing' at life. Academic success does not correlate with senior positions in the workplace later on. Even when girls achieve at school, they opt out of career fast-tracks often because of their commitments to home and family. Regardless of which gender may be seen as 'losing out' in education (or maybe because of the competing messages and consequent debate), gender remains a compelling variable for researchers to examine which factors influence academic success.

There has been an implicit message in schools that girls count less to teachers, which mirrors larger social values concerning male and female, which is also contradicted by the boys' underachievement debate. The message could well reinforce a negative self-image and lead to withdrawal from participation on the part of female students. Research has consistently suggested that boys in classrooms talk more, exert more control over talk and interrupt other speakers more often (Coates, 1993; West & Zimmerman, 1987). In earlier research, girls were assumed to listen more and to be more supportive when they did talk, largely serving as audience to a dynamic largely controlled by boys. Both female and male teachers tended to pay less attention to girls than to boys at all ages, in various socio-economic and ethnic groupings and in all subjects. Girls received less behavioral criticism, fewer instructional contacts, fewer high-level questions and academic criticism and slightly less praise than boys across the age ranges and in all subjects (Graddol & Swann, 1989). Also, there were some reports that found teachers direct more open-ended questions at boys in the early years of schooling, and more yes/no questions at girls (Francis, 2000). It also appears that boys tended to be 'first in' to classroom discussions because of the teachers' own non-verbal cues, particularly their 'gaze-attention', and that this eye contact was important in systematically offering boys more opportunities for participation (Paechter, 1998; Swann, 1992, 1998).

Michael Gurian and Kathy Stevens (2005) published *The Minds of Boys: Saving Our Sons from Falling Behind in School and Life*. Their ideas follow a host of books on the similar them of 'saving' the boys, including Dan Kindlon and Michael Thompson's (1999) *Raising Cain: Protecting the Emotional Life of Boys* and William Pollack's (1998) *Real Boys: Rescuing our Sons from the Myths of Boyhood*. All such books appeal to the worries that weak boys are failures and thus it is imperative to equip boys to be strong and able to succeed. The 'crisis' discourse of lower grades, drop-out rates and lower and later reading levels among boys reinforces the necessity to keep boys on top by appealing to their 'male learning style' and their more physical, aggressive and competitive traits – an essentialist view of masculinity. Such ideas raise the contradictions between the feminist educational discourses. These discussions connect with our vulnerability concerning children.

Our emotional ties to our children are powerful sites of desire: we have dreams, often gendered dreams, for our sons and daughters.

Kindlon and Thompson's (1999) *Raising Cain* taps into the gendered ways we treat boys and how this aligns with the higher risk for suicide, for alcohol and drug abuse, for violence and loneliness. They explore various explanations for these tendencies, including 'mother blame' and 'boy biology', and settle on the way society trains boys to be emotionally disengaged. We see this in the promotion of video games, violent movies and thrill-seeking sports that remove boys from more connected relationships. Kindlon and Thompson call this the 'culture of cruelty' where boys receive little (if any) encouragement to develop qualities such as compassion, sensitivity and warmth. Boys have limited emotional literacy because we, as a society, demand a particular type of masculinity that is success driven and relationally vacant. William Pollack (1998) call this 'the Boy Code' – our demand that boys suppress or cover up their emotions.

The messages (or discourses) are contradictory within educational discussions. On one hand, feminist literature says girls are ignored yet they have a much higher success rate educationally. On the other hand, boys are given far more attention and resources yet continue to be failures. Why is this? Judith Baxter (2003) responds to this with her ideas on post-feminism that see these realities as evidence of the individuality at work in each context. We make choices, consciously or otherwise, to position ourselves in fluid identities.

Much sociolinguistic research has been carried out in classrooms in a search for the explanations underlying basis for gendered speech, and much has been found to solidify the claim that females and males use (or are required to use) language differently, have differing motivations to do so, and that their speech is interpreted differently even when they use the same speech strategies. The examination of male/female differences in classroom interactions and our contradictory expectations and demands of boys and girls in classrooms may be further complicated by context, by power and by different interpretations of the very same linguistic forms when aligned with sex. Nonetheless, certainly some differences appear with regularity across cultures and social groups, highlighting classrooms and schools as key sites for gender rehearsal and performance.

Summary statements

- Gender roles and expectations are prescribed early in life and are accepted and rehearsed by very young children in the school system as stable characteristics.
- Teachers are often unaware of the ways boys and girls are treated in the classroom, believing they 'treat them all the same' when, in fact, boys and girls are responded to in differing ways throughout the school years.
- Silence seems to be a comfortable participation strategy used by female students because more verbal interaction by girls in classrooms is often condemned as 'chatty' and 'trivial'.

Discussion points

With a partner or on your own, consider:

1. Do you think the 'moral panic' surrounding the underachievement of boys is a 'false' concern? Why don't the higher achievement levels of girls in many school systems today and across many subject areas not correlate with lifelong success?

2. Why do you think gender remains a compelling variable to consider when it comes to educational achievement? Why does it matter to us?

3. Would single-sex schools or classrooms help girls or boys with educational success? If classrooms are such 'sites of struggle', could separate single-sexed school populations help everyone in some way?

Further reading

To read more on gender, language use and classroom life or achievement in schooling, see:

Delamont, S. (1990) *Sex Roles and the School* (2nd edn). London: Routledge.

Epstein, D., Elwood, J., Hey, V. and Maw, J. (eds) (1998) *Failing Boys? Issues in Gender and Achievement*. Buckingham: Open University Press.

Francis, B. (2005) *Reassessing Gender and Achievement: Questioning Key Debates*. London: Routledge.

Jule, A. (2004) *Gender and Silence in a Language Classroom: Sh-shushing the Girls*. Basingstoke: Palgrave Macmillan.

Kramarae, C. and Triechler, P. (1990) Power relationships in the classroom. In S. Gabriel and I. Smithson (eds) *Gender in the Classroom: Power and Pedagogy* (pp. 41–59). Chicago: University of Illinois Press.

Paechter, C. (1998) *Educating the Other: Gender, Power and Schooling*. London: Falmer.

Sheldon, A. (1997) Talking power: Girls, gender enculturation and discourse. In R. Wodak (ed.) *Gender and Discourse* (pp. 225–44). London: Sage.

Skelton, C., Francis B. and Smylyan, L. (2006) *The Sage Handbook of Gender and Education*. London: Sage

Swann, J. (1992) *Girls, Boys, and Language*. Oxford: Blackwell.

5

Gender and language use in the workplace

This chapter explores some of the complexities of the workplace and how gender and language use connect to create specific tensions and freedoms by asking these key questions:

- How do the 'deficit/dominance' or 'difference' paradigms influence the ways we perceive gender in the workplace?

- Why has 'women's language' emerged into 'women's style of leadership'? And why is there no such thing?

- Why is leadership and authority usually understood as 'masculine'?

- What is the glass ceiling and why does it matter to us who holds the most powerful positions in society?

- Why is it that highly educated boys have consistently the most successful careers, while highly educated girls do not?

- Why do able women 'opt out' of their careers? Why don't men do so for similar reasons?

'The trouble with being in the rat race is that even if you win you're still a rat.'
Lily Tomlin, American actress (1939–)

Early research examining language and gender in the workplace was heavily influenced by popular paradigms at the time, namely the deficit and dominance approaches to gender (see Chapter 2). As women began to enter the workplace, language and gender research in this area started to grow and a number of key studies were produced. Early studies took differences in gender as a given and as a way of constructing identities to some extent. Some studies focused on the domain of medicine, such as doctor–patient interactions (West, 1984, 1990); women police officers (McElhinny, 1998); and women in courts of law (O'Barr & Atkins, 1998) and more recent research uses the social constructionist lens to interpret conversations at work. Ultimately, research in this area seems to contradict a gender binary and simplistic theorizations of gender.

Nevertheless and according to many of these studies, the power that men are seen to have over women in society is often reconstructed in their workplace encounters, and research examines the linguistic strategies that women and men adopt in both single and mixed-sex settings at work. There has been a huge growth in work that examines gender and communicative strategies among colleagues, particularly in business (see Baxter, 2003; Holmes, 2006). This chapter highlights some significant studies and lingering issues necessary to understand gender and language use in the workplace.

Framing gender in workplace relationships

By the mid-1990s, social constructionist approaches to language and gender began to develop alongside difference theory. In addition to the notions of 'doing gender', some, such as Shari Kendall and Deborah Tannen (1997), have drawn on the notion of 'framing' as helpful in understanding various interactions. Women and men often 'frame' themselves and others based on societal gendered norms for appropriate behavior. Kendall and Tannen argue that the relationship between language and gender is 'sex-class' linked; that is, spoken interaction is not necessarily identified with a woman or man but is rather associated with 'women as a class' or 'men as a class' within society – as a subculture. Individuals align themselves with a particular sex-class by talking in a particular way.

Discursive and social constructionist approaches have been particularly important in workplace studies in recent years. Studies by Janet Holmes and her colleagues are good examples of such approaches. In 1996, Holmes set up a government-funded project in Wellington, New Zealand, entitled *Language and the Workplace*. Early publications associated with this project demonstrate the transition in language and gender studies away from the dominance and difference paradigms of the 1970s and 1980s to the more dynamic 'communities of practice' social constructionist approaches (Holmes, 2000). Holmes's work is important because it argues that it is not possible to make generalizations about the behavior of 'women' versus 'men' at work because there are a myriad of complexities, particular roles, professional identities and social contexts that influence each interaction.

While there may be some evidence of gendered patterning, there is also more and more compelling evidence that gendered interactional styles may be stereotypically 'true' but are in no way universal. It is not always the case that a feminine style of leadership is more indirect, conciliatory, facilitative or collaborative, or that a masculine style is more direct, aggressive, competitive and autonomous. Holmes's analysis of the speech strategies of women managers in positions of power found that they were using a 'wide-verbal-repertoire style' (Holmes, 2000: 13). The women studied displayed traits stereotypically associated with both masculine and feminine speech styles. All the women managers Holmes examined were evaluated as being effective by their colleagues, regardless of their sex. Holmes attributes workplace success to a mixture of stereotypical masculine and feminine discourse styles that the women managers in her study used to achieve their goals. Many argue that a full repertoire of styles with both men and women displaying characteristics stereotypically associated with masculine and feminine speech, enables participants to be simultaneously assertive and supportive. Both styles are effective for both sexes depending on their transactional and relational goals.

Louise Mullany (2003) examined gendered discourses in interviews with female and male managers at middle and senior managerial levels in Britain. One of her aims was to discuss participants' managerial roles and the impact of gender on their everyday work lives. The results suggested that women in positions of authority are often evaluated negatively, even in spite of their success in their jobs. Mullany suggests that this is in large part due to the ideal of femininity that centers around physical appearance rather than competence. Only when women look the 'right' way for the job are they viewed positively. The women themselves were very aware of this as the requirement for success and felt trapped by it. The view perpetuated by the dominant discourse of femininity regarding the feminine

image appears to be that women need to be slim, attractive and well-groomed to be taken seriously in the workplace.

There is also the discourse of female emotionality that plays a part of gender in the workplace. Mullany's interviews record men articulating stereotypical views about that 'one week a month' when women are more emotional and therefore incapable of being rational at work. That so many men in Mullany's study spoke to this and did so in very matter-of-fact ways suggests that perhaps many men view this as common sense.

Others, such as Lazar (2005), have argued that gender in the workplace reveals a deeply embedded androcentrism in which both men and women are complicit. Even if professionals see the skills of men and women as interchangeable in positions at work, there is a rationalization that individuality is the main cause of success or failure. It seems that gender can be used as an excuse for some and viewed as a non-issue by others.

The glass ceiling

Regardless of the ways in which men and women have been linguistically framed by gendered identities and regardless of the use of both masculine and feminine speech styles in successful leaders at work, it has been the case that more men succeed in the traditional world of business and workplace settings. That women rarely achieve top levels of senior leadership is known as not breaking through the glass ceiling.

According to Sally McConnell-Ginet (2000: 260), the glass ceiling is:

The invisible barrier that seems to keep even some exceptionally capable women from ascending to the top in many professions dominated by men. Its companion, the glass elevator, is the invisible leverage that propels even relatively mediocre men upward in female-dominated occupations.

The glass ceiling is primarily about two things: visibility and power, and not separately but in combination. It seems to be the case that, in spite of the many feminist advances concerning education and gender equity laws, there are fewer women who have access to real power or exercise visible power in the workplace. It is fine for women (and other minorities) to be visible in various places of business as long as they don't have any meaningful or serious power. There are plenty of women who serve as vice-presidents or vice-principals but fewer who are presidents of major companies or heads of major educational institutions. That is

to say, women are in important jobs but they are essentially in supportive jobs. It seems okay for women to have power, as long as they are behind the scenes and not exercising that power too visibly. For example, women comprise 46.5% of the American workforce but hold only 12% of upper management level positions (Wichterich, 2000). Similar trends are seen in countries around the world.

There is a tendency to consider the issue of gender parity as only a recent concern. But David Graddol and Joan Swann (1989) and Peggy Eckert and Sally McConnell-Ginet (2003) argue that gender ideologies have long worked to ensure that the same speech style is given a different meaning and interpretation when used by a woman rather than a man. It has been only about 30 years since women have been promoted and invited into roles of leadership so that research in workplace contexts are recent. Women have always worked outside the domestic spheres, but it seems that, regardless of competency or education, a woman can only go so far. The existence of some success stories does not eliminate the fact that the workplace is not a level playing field when it comes to male:female ratios. Women earn less for similar work: in general, women earn 70 cents for every dollar a man earns; while in the US, female academics earn $10,000 less per year than their male colleagues (Wichterich, 2000).

To have both women and men in various kinds of employment, including top positions of leadership, means that both aspiring men and women can see success as genderless. It means a lot to see women (as well as other ethnic minorities) at the top of their field. When role models do achieve in some way but are then treated unjustly in another way (or are seen to be treated unjustly), there is a profoundly negative effect on entire communities and those coming along behind. The lack of women in both real and visible positions of power is more than a token of unfairness. When women are blocked from fully participating in society it violates basic human rights. It is, therefore, important to consider why some women are excluded – why so many hit the glass ceiling in various career paths and how women are represented. A blockage to leadership is made evident in language use: both what is said to limit women and what is understood by the women themselves (Crawford, 1995; Mullany, 2003).

Gender at work

Today's young women in the Western world rank among the most educated in history, yet many also grapple with frustrations never imagined by their mothers or grandmothers. Canadian researchers, Lesley Andres and Harvey Krahn (1999), for example, gathered 15 years of data on Canadian youth's transition to adulthood. They studied 700 people, both men and women, as they moved their way through early adulthood to work, marriage and having children. Their work suggests that Canadian women, despite having earned comparable post-secondary credentials, are twice as likely as men to be employed part-time, pooling in the clerical, sales and services sector. In contrast, men work primarily in middle management and as semi-professionals or professionals. Highly educated boys have consistently the most successful career trajectories over highly educated girls who often 'opt-out' of a career path to bear or tend children at a critical stage in career development.

Stereotyping and preconceptions of women are also two of the biggest barriers women face at work – not blatant sexism but outdated ideas rooted in stereotypes about women's abilities and commitment to their careers. Other obstacles include exclusion from informal networks of communication (such as the golf club) and a lack of mentors. Women often feel excluded from casual and social settings (having drinks, going for lunch) where deals are discussed and networking happens. A senior man seems more likely to take a younger man under his wing and introduce him to important people. Women, however, are often left to navigate the political waters on their own. Many women 'opt-out' even when they have opportunities because of the lifestyle decisions necessary in achieving and holding positions of power (Women's Media, 2003). Also, according to Canada's Women's Media, at least 50% of women have experienced sexual harassment at work. Sexual harassment can take many linguistic forms, including propositions, jokes, suggestive comments, innuendo and comments about appearance. It also seems to be a vicious circle: women experience more frustration and exclusion in positions of leadership so they 'opt-out', leaving fewer women in the workplace to mentor and guide others. Women opt-out and thus feed the view that women can't (or won't) handle pressure at work.

As a place of business, it is worth commenting on the role of women in academia. Perhaps it is no surprise that scholars in the field would turn the lens on their own workplaces. British, American, Australian and Canadian universities cite similar trends of more women academics entering the profession. However, women's jobs in academia tend to be more junior, more teaching-based, more pastoral and often part-time.

Sally McConnell-Ginet (2000) wonders if, when achievement is rewarded, men get credit for determination and commitment, while women are seen as lucky and having to work extraordinarily hard to fulfill the task. Claire Walsh (2001) found that women's increased presence in traditionally male-dominated workplaces such as academia has resulted in a 'strengthening of fraternal networks' and a blocking out of women. Also, Barbara Reskin and Patricia Roos (1990) claim that women typically enter fields that men no longer find desirable due to loss of pay, prestige or autonomy. This possibility may help to explain women in junior positions within academia – men don't want the extra burden of teaching positions, so women can have them. Such explanations may also help explain the increase of women in the medical profession and in the clergy over the last 30 years as well. Alternatively, Reskin and Roos see men entering certain jobs once viewed as only for women, like nursing, as raising the status of the job.

Style of leadership

Women at work is a complicated issue. We have been raised in a binary of female/male that has created distinct gendered worlds for us. Women seem to be associated with certain attributes, such as the ability to share power and information, to multi-task and to build consensus. But these are positive traits regardless of one's sex (Cameron, 2001; Holmes, 2006). Companies are increasingly valuing the blending of various leadership styles. Even so, men are often selected for top jobs based on perceived potential rather than actual performance and because their leadership style is seen as more authoritative, commanding and confident.

Whether women are fluent in cooperative styles or not, researchers such as Lia Litosseliti (2006) see that the assumptions of gender positions are powerful. Especially in male-dominated workplaces – business organizations, government, politics, the Church, the police, the law – where assertive behavior is necessary, women must constantly negotiate gender assumptions and expectations. For example, Bonnie McElhinny (1998) explores how women police officers tend to 'masculinize' their behaviour and refrain from cooperative strategies in order to be effective.

According to Litosseliti, the appropriation of 'masculine' styles by women in such communities is understandable, given the historical context of struggle for women to gain access to certain roles. Because of this, Litosseliti believes that women often adopt interactional approaches that align with leadership styles in certain workplaces. Judith Baxter's (2006) collection of research on the female voice in public contexts provides insight on how women both appropriate masculine public discourse and find new ways of combining 'doing leadership' and 'doing gender' successfully.

Some studies have looked at gender tendencies in leadership. For example, Mintzberg's (1973) study found that men in business tended to:

1. work at an unrelenting pace, with no breaks in activity during the day;
2. give way to interruption, discontinuity and fragmentation;
3. spare little time for activities not directly related to their work;
4. establish a preference for live action encounters;
5. maintain a complex network of relationships with people outside of their organization (peers, colleagues, clients for the purposes of information gathering);
6. immerse themselves in the day-to-day need to keep the company going, but they lacked time for reflection;
7. identify themselves with their jobs (strong identity to job role);
8. have difficulty sharing information (information as power and they were reluctant to share the information, causing overburdened workloads because the decisions always required them).

Sally Helgesen (1995) revisited Mintzberg's study and examined women's style of leadership. In contrast, she found that women tended to:

1. work at a steady pace, but with small breaks throughout the day (used the breaks for returning phone calls or following up on tasks);
2. not view unscheduled tasks and encounters as interruptions but as key to the working of the business (the women used words like caring, being involved, helping and being responsible);
3. take time for activities not directly related to their work;
4. prefer live action encounters, but scheduled time to attend to mail;
5. maintain a complex network of relationships with people outside their organizations;
6. focus on the ecology of leadership (kept to a long-term focus);
7. see their own identities as complex and multi-faceted;
8. schedule in time for sharing information.

What is worth considering is the demands on those in leadership positions and the unrelenting pressures in capitalist societies for success.

The drive for gendered success can limit men's connection to their families and communities as well as limit women from the fulfillment that can come from using one's training and talent for the larger world. The distinct gender styles and experiences have both benefits and limitations for men and women alike.

Summary statements

- Studies show that positions of influence in our society (such as medicine, law, politics, business) attract men who are trained to lead and are more comfortable with positions that require authoritative leadership styles of communicating.
- Even while today's women are the most educated in history, many opt-out of top positions because combining work life and home life is too difficult or exhausting to manage.
- The glass ceiling causes not just a personal loss for some women, it influences everyone by keeping women from visibility and influence. This has negative consequences for both women and men by limiting human aspirations.

Discussion points

With a partner or on your own, consider:

1. Are there particular ways in which women and men interact at work that limit success? Is success itself seen in highly gendered ways?

2. If women 'opt-out' of top levels of governance and leadership, why is this seen as part of the glass ceiling? If women make their own choice not to climb the corporate ladder, why does this matter to society-at-large?

3. If both 'feminine' and 'masculine' styles of speaking and leading are useful and even desired in the workplace, why is the workforce so gendered? Why do more women do more care-centered work while men do more technical work?

Further reading

For more on gender, language and the workplace, I suggest:

Baxter, J. (ed.) (2006) *Speaking Out: The Female Voice in Public Contexts*. Basingstoke: Palgrave Macmillan.

Helgesen, S. (1995) *The Female Advantage*. New York: Doubleday.

Holmes, J. (2006) *Gendered Talk at Work: Constructing Gender Identity through Workplace Discourse*. Oxford: Blackwell.

Kendall, S. and Tannen, D. (1997) Gender and language in the workplace. In R. Wodak (ed.) *Gender and Discourse* (pp. 81–105). New York: Longman.

McConnell-Ginet, S. (2000) Breaking through the glass ceiling: Can linguistic awareness help? In J. Holmes (ed.) *Gendered Speech in Social Context: Perspectives from Gown to Town* (pp. 259–82). Wellington: Victoria University Press.

Reskin, B. and Roos, P. (eds) (1990) *Job Queues, Gender Queues: Explaining Women's Inroads Into Male Occupations*. Philadelphia: Temple University Press.

Tannen, D. (1995) *Talking from 9 to 5*. London: Virago.

6

Gender and language use in the Western Church

Using the Christian Church as a prime case study, this chapter explores how religious views and attitudes connect with gender and language use by asking these key questions:

- In what ways is Christianity's relationship to the West connected to cultural views of gender roles?

- Does the notion of God as male and the speaking of God in masculine ways matter to those in the Church? How so?

- How do egalitarians and complementarians explain gender roles inside Christianity, particularly in reference to the man as 'head' of the woman? Why the heated debate?

- Are there gender 'differences' in morality that could be seen in all religious communities?

- Is religion itself misogynist or has scripture been interpreted by adherents in misogynist ways?

'A woman's asking for equality in the church would be comparable to a black person demanding equality in the Ku Klux Klan.'
Mary Daly, American theologian (1928–)

In today's global pluralism, almost any faith can be found anywhere, both as a presence and as an option of personal religious persuasion. Hinduism, Buddhism and Islam (religions originating in the East) are found all over the West, and the various representations of the West's Judaism and Christianity are now well established throughout the world. What interests me about the Christian Church is its peculiar status as both an institution and a symbol of personal faith for many, particularly in the West. The massive rise in American-style right-wing evangelical Christianity has been a fascinating sociological phenomenon for some time – both in the US and in other countries around the world. Because of this, the connections of gender and language with a particular religious expression make for a fascinating case study.

The Christian Church has been challenged from within about the differential gendered roles of women and men, as well as women's ordination and gay rights. Since many people have had some connection with a religious tradition of some sort, it is worthwhile to consider the ways in which gender and language use connect with religion, whether this connection is with Christianity or with another faith entirely. This chapter considers some of the ways in which language and gender have connected with the traditional Christian Church and, by extension, how we, as a society, have absorbed its messages concerning gender.

In March 2007, the Canadian Anglican bishop Michael Ingham called for a 'new theology of human sexuality' (Valpy, 2007: A3). He told a large Church conference that the Church's opposition to birth control, abortion, masturbation and homosexuality has been 'morally groundless'. He cited embedded patriarchy in the Church as a 'distortion of the gospel'.

Angela McRobbie (1994: 112) suggests that 'the Church [exists] alongside the pressure groups, the charities, and the voluntary organizations which, when taken as a whole, represent a strong body of public opinion'. This is particularly evident in the United States where there are now at least 70 million evangelical Christians making this particular evangelicalism the most popular religious subgroup in the Western world. Also, worldwide, the number of religious believers of various faiths are increasing. Even in the midst of secularism, religious faith remains relevant for many, maybe even for most (Meyerhoff, 2005). It is also somewhat bewildering that the foundational religion of the West has both promoted equality as well as denied it. Because Christianity has had so much influence in the establishment of Western society, it is important for us as scholars to consider implications for the field of language and gender.

Notions of God as male

Women have experienced a long history of segregation and subordination within the institutional structures of the Christian Church. Two main views of women exist today: complementarian and egalitarian. Both views accept that women have long played a secondary role in Church life, but the disagreement emerges from the view of this role in the faith community and whether it is central to the Christian faith or something culturally developed. Complementarians argue that men should exercise authority or power both in the Church and in family life, thereby placing women in supportive roles; by contrast, egalitarians see women and men as equally able to contribute to the Church and in the family. Complementarians use scripture and 2000 years of Church history to support the exclusion of women from the top levels of Church governance: women, instead, are to complement men's roles. On the other hand, egalitarians highlight historical examples of women in Church leadership (early mystics and prophets, for example) and cite scriptures that support the equal status of women. Egalitarians see the secondary role of women in the Church as cultural, not scriptural.

Much of the debate on the role of women within the Christian Church has involved the creating of a new vision of language use, including traditional hymns and the Bible itself. Keeping in mind the patriarchal culture in which the Bible emerged some 2000 years ago, some of today's feminist scholars have searched for and found passages and images supportive of an equal position for women. They hold the egalitarian view that female oppression in the Church has been a reflection of a misogynist culture, not at all connected to holiness or godliness. They focus on the Bible's teaching that all of humanity is created equal in God's image. Feminist scholars have also offered new ways to understand some apparently patriarchal passages. Because they understand 'God' to be acting in both 'masculine' and 'feminine' ways, it is possible to conceive of God as both male *and* female. Egalitarians hold to this view, but complementarians do not. They see gender hierarchy as part of 'God's order' of things: women are created by God to support good men.

Theologian Mary Daly (1973) believed that the reference to God as 'Our Father' has been disastrous – a product of human imagination that limits women's ability to fully contribute to the world around them. Deborah Cameron (1995: 4) also attacks women's exclusion from full participation in Church life, saying 'it is not just that women do not speak: often they are explicitly *prevented* from speaking, either by social taboos and restrictions or by the more genteel tyrannies of custom and practice'.

It is no secret that male scholars have had a monopoly on Christian discourse. Evangelical churches in particular have relied on scriptural arguments about the 'headship' of men based on the view of God's order of creation: man first, then woman (see Genesis 2). Once women entered the field of theology in the 1970s, they were in positions to promote other scriptures declaring the equality of all people. Claire Walsh (2001: 167) points to the use of certain scriptural passages over others as a 'site of ideological struggle, with a complex set of competing readings becoming polarized along gender lines'. There are basically two wings of the Church: evangelicals who are mainly complementarians and liberals who are mainly egalitarians. Both sides of the debate see their interpretation as central to their faith. Women are either as central as men or they have different roles to play than men; this is not a both/and situation but an either/or one.

The strength of the understanding of the male as central within Christianity is most evident in the belief of an unbroken male line from Jesus through his apostles to their successors. A male priest is standing in for Christ: the maleness of the priest is not incidental but theologically essential. But this view is problematic for women, and some have left the Church over it. Daly, for example, left the Church because of it, declaring: 'Since God is male, then the male *is* God'. According to this analysis, the Christian faith is a location of and even a defence for patriarchy. For some, patriarchy is a God-given order, while for others it is a human evil that must be stopped.

Some devoted Christians stay out of the debate entirely because of what they see to be more pressing social concerns such as poverty, the environment and domestic abuse. However, failure to recognize that these social concerns are also often linked to gender marginalizes women even further. Many, such as Rebecca Chopp (1989), believe that the rise in women's roles in the Church is related to the diminished standing of the Church in the West. Now that there is a crisis in manpower, the Church needs women and has begun to find ways to explain and promote their service. One of the most observable influences of feminism on Christianity in the last 30 years is the increased number of women in positions of leadership within the Church. Even so, their presence reveals the traditional power discrepancies and views of gender. Many women clergy express their frustrations with their roles and their lack of legitimacy. Being male still equates with public displays of faith and influence, while being female equates with a more private, supportive expression of faithfulness (Connell, 1995; Gilligan, 1982). Even women in Church leadership cannot veer too far off the feminine behaviors of gentleness, nurturing and thoughtfulness.

Like many egalitarian campaigners for women's ordination within the Christian church, Monica Furlong (1991) saw the campaign to have **gender-inclusive language**, such as the use of 's/he' rather than the so-called generic 'he', and 'people' rather than 'man', accepted as central to the feminist project of securing equality for men and women in the Church. A change of language could indicate the Church's attitudes to women. But there have been objections. Some see inclusive language as problematic because it leads to a 'lack of dignity', a 'weakening of sense', and 'a diluting of the richness' in ancient scriptures and hymns (Thomas, 1996: 168). Such debates continue in most Christian denominations with various effects. In fact, almost every church has had to come to some understanding about inclusive language, and the majority of views align with the egalitarian view concerning the oppression of women.

Gender-neutral language and scripture

Gender-neutral language is a style of writing that adheres to certain 'rules' that were first proposed by feminists in the 1970s. These rules prohibit common usages that are deemed to be sexist, such as the word 'chairman'. But in Christian theology, there are trickier problems. For example, God is often described in the Bible as 'the God of Abraham, Isaac, and Jacob' (see Exodus 3:16), but not 'the God of Sarah, Rebekah, and Rachel'. What do theologians do with the scriptures that do privilege the male experience? Another example is the book of Proverbs. It is entirely addressed to young men seeking wisdom but no advice is directly given to women.

There are examples of similar androcentrism in the New Testament as well. For example, in I Corinthians 14:34, St. Paul says that women 'should keep silent' in the church. Women are told to 'be subject to your husbands as to the Lord' (Ephesians 5:22–24). In short, the Bible is not gender-neutral but rather gender-specific. To change the language of patriarchy in the Bible may only disguise the misogyny embedded in it. Changing the language will not necessarily remove the patriarchal bias because the patterns and images are arguably part of our subconscious. Some feminist theologians have demanded the removal of the most explicitly misogynist passages but with little effect because the canonicity is too entrenched. Even if their hopes were realized, there may be little effect (see Carson, 1998, for a fuller discussion).

Recent events in the evangelical community – particularly the release of a gender-inclusive Bible, the TNIV translation (Today's New International Version, 2002) – have raised new concerns over gender and language. For example, does Jesus ask his followers to be fishers of people or fishers of men (Matthew 4:19)? Is there a difference? Christian women have constantly needed to ask themselves if Biblical references to 'man', 'men', 'him' actually include them. Other phrases in traditional Christian hymns such as 'Good Christian Men Rejoice' or 'Rise Up, O Men of God' are similarly problematic. Many hymns were written before gender issues entered public consciousness but their continued use raises concerns. In many cases, we are to assume 'men' is used generically to include everyone – but feminist scholars question the assumptions themselves: some aspects of the faith include women but others do not. Some instructions seem to be given to both men and women, but some only to women and some only to men (see Jule, 2005).

Other concerns related to gender-inclusive language within the Christian Church focus the metaphors used for God. Some metaphors such as 'rock' and 'fortress' are abstract and poetic; others, such as 'father' and 'son', are anthropomorphic or personal or masculine. Feminist theologians wonder why feminine metaphors have not been emphasized, since they have also been used throughout the Bible. For example, the Old Testament refers to God as 'a mother bird' (Psalm 17:8b), 'a mother bear' (Hosea 13:8a) and 'a midwife' (Psalm 22:9). There are numerous similar examples of God being portrayed as feminine throughout the Christian scriptures; but, perhaps more important is an understanding of God as both transcendent and removed from human gender limitations. If God is limitless, then using human metaphors to explain the nature of God will always be problematic. That is to say, God is neither male nor female, but both masculine and feminine. Metaphorical references to God are not absolutes, but rather poetic abstractions used to conceive of God in understandable terms. God is no more female than God is male – but not all Christians agree on this point.

Gender and expressions of morality

In her influential book, *In a Different Voice*, Carol Gilligan (1982) explored gendered language patterns, including gendered patterns of expressing morality. For Gilligan, morality appears closely, if not entirely, connected with one's sense of obligation and one's view of personal sacrifice. She suggests that masculine morality is generally concerned with the public world of social performance and influence, while feminine morality is more often concerned with the private and personal realm. As a result, the moral judgments and moral behaviors and expressions of men tend to differ from those of women. In this way, Gilligan ascribes to gender as difference perspective. However, in light of Gilligan's ideas, I would suggest that individuals participating in an evangelical subculture are often encouraged to perform gender in such a way as to connect masculine behavior to public displays of influence and feminine behavior to more intimate, private displays. Evangelical men are rehearsed into the role of performer; while evangelical women are rehearsed into the role of silent audience member. Women's silence demonstrates to others and to the women themselves a devoutness to God, as seen in their ability to be supportive. Their silence is their way of being good.

One might have thought that the current increased participation of women in Christian theological education, the rise of feminist theology and the growth of women's ordination would have significantly changed the nature of theological education in particular. However, recent research into the lives of evangelical women who chose theological education indicates that the lived experiences of these women are often painful and confusing (Gallagher, 2003; Ingersoll, 2003; Mutch, 2003). With various other religious experiences possible (including none at all), some women appear to remain and invest in their evangelical subculture because they experience something meaningful and worthwhile (Jule, 2006). Women who study theology say they are often dismissed as working against their own purposes, as anti-woman, for pursuing theology and are often marginalized as a result of this label. Still others feel marginalized and limited and nervous about their possible future contributions to Church life; they anticipate problems even if they have not yet experienced any (Mutch, 2003). Canadian women in theological education report that being a woman in ministry requires 'commitment of conviction' which is carried out within a constant 'context of challenge' (Busse, 1998). Most cite both loneliness and stress as elements of their career choice. Nevertheless, women continue to enrol in theological education, to graduate and to go on to seek ordination. They choose such struggle. My own research at a theological college revealed how quiet women are in some Christian settings and how their reasons for this are connected to their religious identity (Jule, 2005).

Many researchers have undertaken studies on the relationship of evangelical Christian faith and femininity, most recently Susan Gallagher (2003) and Julie Ingersoll (2003). Both of these scholars offer compelling evidence concerning gender roles and expectations in the evangelical sub-culture, and both suggest that evangelicalism appears a salient religious experience to many, even with (or perhaps because of) the necessary adherence to traditional Christian teachings concerning gender roles. Evangelicalism's ability to thrive in the midst of larger secularism and current religious pluralism is in part because it is a religious subculture that appears to accommodate cultural engagement along with conservative theological orthodoxy (Gallagher, 2003).

The 1980s and 1990s saw anti-feminism emerge in American society, specifically inside evangelical circles (what Susan Faludi, 1993, called the 'backlash'). And in spite of early feminist claims made by mostly evangelical women in the 1800s and early 1900s, the current American Christian 'right' asserts political pressure on issues concerning the family in direct opposition to feminist causes. It seems that now evangelicals articulate a view of society that rejects liberalism and equality in favor of certainty and moral conservatism. Their views emerge from a belief that men lead as benign but clear patriarchs who can and must insulate their families from the complexity of secular life, while women serve as supporters of their efforts (Gallagher, 2003). As a result, many evangelical men and women believe they achieve morality and a resulting peace of mind by behaving in stereotypically masculine and feminine ways: men to lead, women to submit to male leadership and to male significance.

Sally Gallagher (2003) suggests that women remain in Christian Church life and even choose careers within the Church precisely because of the set roles for women, not in spite of them. Such women find the clarity 'empowering' (p. 11). The rhetoric of a strong masculine Christianity appeals to men as well as to many women. Even organizations within Christianity that support and promote female ordination do so within the set dogma, offering differing interpretations of key scriptures concerning the role of women but not differing interpretations of gendered behavior. Men are to be strong and rational, and women are to support male 'headship', even if they are ordained and in the positions of leadership. Though some women may have difficulty in such a context, many appear to remain and further invest themselves precisely because of a sense of belonging.

They work out their gender roles within a specific framework of male leadership and domination.

The relationship of religion, any religion, with genderedness is politically fascinating. Words and images used for God reflect a particular understanding of the Divine. Those who have a religious faith (Christian or otherwise) often connect notions of goodness with gender so that masculinity is often viewed as initiating and even redeeming while femininity is viewed as receptive. Does religious faith relate goodness to specific gender performances? If there are gendered ways to be moral, are there also gendered ways to be immoral? And what does this tell us about our view of spirituality and humanness? The specific use of certain words, phrases and textual interpretation of scriptures link to such views. In addition, the ways people speak in religious communities connect with genderedness, making religious groups and religious identities remain a compelling site within which to explore gender and language use.

Summary statements

- Christianity (as well as other faith communities) works alongside gender identity in particular ways, influencing the views of gender inclusion or exclusion and influencing gendered behaviors of belonging.
- Both Christian scripture and tradition support both the oppression and the liberation of women: either view can be promoted as 'true'.
- Though women participate in Christian Church leadership and governance, the priesthood and ministry have been mainly male-dominated, which has influenced the interpretation of scriptures as well as the promotion of androcentric imagery.

Discussion points

With a partner or on your own, consider:

1. In your own experience, do you see religion as having influenced aspects of your genderedness? Or has your genderedness influenced your religious views? How might religious ceremonies (such as a wedding) celebrate particular gender roles and behaviors?

2. Does it matter to those outside a religion how women inside it are treated? Do religious people and their views influence the whole of society or just their religious communities?

3. In what ways might Christianity in particular help explain the legacy of patriarchy in Western culture? Are all religions sexist to some extent?

Further reading

To explore more on gender, language and the debates in the Christian Church regarding gender roles, see:

Chopp, R. (1989) *The Power to Speak: Feminism, Language and God.* New York: Crossroad.

Gallagher, S. K. (2003) *Evangelical Identity and Gendered Family Life.* London: Rutgers University Press.

Hancock, M. (ed.) (2003) *Christian Perspectives on Gender, Sexuality, and Community.* Vancouver: Regent College Publishing.

Ingersoll, J. (2003) *Evangelical Christian Women: War Stories in the Gender Battles.* New York: New York University Press.

Jule, A. and Pedersen, B. (eds) (2006) *Being Feminist, Being Christian: Essays from Academia.* New York: Palgrave.

Storkey, E. (2001) *Origins of Difference: The Gender Debate Revisited.* Grand Rapids, MI: Baker Book House Company.

Walsh, C. (2001) *Gender and Discourse: Language and Power in Politics, the Church and Organizations.* London: Pearson Education.

7

Gender and language use in relationships

This chapter explores how language use serves as a tool to both create as well as maintain personal relationships by asking these key questions:

- How is language used for the establishment of relationships?

- In what ways is 'difference theory' used to explain how men and women form their own subcultures, forming in early childhood in same-sex peer groups? How do these subcultures serve as sites of belonging and/or as exclusion?

- What does 'the second shift' tell us about the myth of family patterns?

- How does language use align with gendered roles to position participants inside families and friendship groups?

- In what ways are 'friendship sites' interpreted through assumptions about gender?

'Sometimes I wonder if men and women really suit each other. Perhaps they should live next door and just visit now and then.'
Katharine Hepburn, Hollywood icon (1907–2003)

Traditionally, researchers of sociolinguistics in general as well as language and gender have necessarily distinguished between what is known as institutional talk, and what is regarded as ordinary, everyday language. In the workplace, in classrooms or in other public places, language is often oriented to a goal or task of some sort. But at home and in more personal relationships, language is used for the establishment and maintenance of relationships. This chapter explores the role of social talk in personal relationships, and the ways in which language and gender relate and are used in friendships and in family life.

The role of social talk

Bonnie McElhinny (1998) problematizes the dichotomy of 'ordinary' vs 'institutional' language that is commonly used in sociolinguistic research. She links public and private contexts and emphasizes 'the separation rather than the interpenetration of spheres' (p. 108). McElhinny demonstrates that this distinction between public and private gets blurry in certain circumstances. Social talk (at home and in one's personal relationships) is in many ways 'ordinary talk'; yet many workplaces rely on this more casual and friendly style to achieve work-related goals, and many personal relationships also function as task-groups. Deborah Tannen (1991) describes social talk used in places of business to create rapport among staff for the purposes of conducting effective business. Also, Shari Kendall (2004) explores how female managers tend to use social talk honed in their personal relationships to create a relaxed work environment. Both Tannen (1995) and Janet Holmes (2003) consider how higher-ranking women tell stories at work to sustain authority by framing and positioning their identities as more personal. To some extent, social talk creates rapport and negotiates the status of participants in personal relationships in particular.

Eleanor Maccoby (1990) suggests that sex differences only emerge in primarily social situations. In early childhood, children find same-sex partners more compatible. As children move into adolescence, the patterns they developed in their childhood same-sex groups are carried over into cross-sex encounters, whereas girls' interactive styles put them at a disadvantage. Maccoby found that gender segregation is a widespread phenomenon found in all cultures. Preschool children spend a great deal of their time engaged in activities that are gender neutral but, as they age, their interests diverge along gender lines. Why does this happen? Maccoby suggests that 'peer groups are the setting in which children first discover the compatibility of same-sex others, in which boys first discover the requirements of maintaining one's status in the male hierarchy, and in which the gender of one's partners becomes supremely important' (p. 519).

In mixed-gendered conversation, the variation in speaking style can lead to misunderstandings. A woman talking to a male friend may interpret his infrequent positive minimal responses as a sign that he is not interested in what she is saying, while to him, this means that he does not always agree with her. On the other hand, a man receiving frequent nods and 'mhms' from his female interlocutor may interpret this as a sign of agreement. To her, it may merely indicate that she is listening. Daniel Maltz and Ruth Borker (1998) use this example to help explain a common complaint in male–female interaction: men think women agree with them but later change their minds, while women think men don't listen to them. Maltz and Borker conclude that there are 'two separate rules for conversation maintenance which come into conflict and cause massive miscommunication' (p. 422). This view aligns with the difference theory – that men and women form their own subcultures, subcultures that form during childhood in same-sex peer groups. Maltz and Borker suggest that these conversation patterns are 'learned in childhood and carried over into adulthood as the bases for patterns of single-sex friendship relations and ... miscommunication in cross-sex interaction' (p. 423). Women's conversation is interactional; men's is more hierarchical, more story-telling and verbal posturing.

Rachel Rafelman (1997) reported in *Toronto Life* magazine how it is that men and women divide along gender lines in social settings and how both men and women find women more interesting to talk to at parties, specifically because of many women's more developed interactive style. Rafelman refers to women as 'the social grease people' because of their 'training' in drawing people out and getting others to talk about themselves. Rafelman also points out that women rarely assert themselves in mixed social settings and so males often dominate these conversations. From early childhood, females are spoken to differently than males and so the content of their speech is often 'soft' and their opinions are expressed more obliquely. Even highly confident women temper their speech with backchannel support ('Oh really' and 'How fascinating'). They nod, smile a lot and keep their gaze on the speaker's face. Rafelman says that this works 'very well' and, hence, women continue to develop this style. Listening is an important aspect of 'girl talk' since it is at the center of reciprocal communication throughout the lives of many women.

Participating in family life

We all create and maintain certain roles for a variety of purposes: there is diversity in our ways of participating in the various relationships in our lives. Kendall (2006) argues that at each moment in any encounter, we take up, resist and assign positions by locating ourselves and others in relation to various values or characteristics, including such social categories as mother or father or sister or son. There are various discourses and ways of speaking and behaving. There are also different topics and subject positions available in different family groupings. We participate in relationships at home because of the available positions we hold. We may speak in certain ways and about certain things in one role (say, as a daughter) and then quite differently and about different topics altogether in another role (say, as a mother).

Kendall (2006) also points to the role of caregiver as often in the hands of a woman. The archetype is based on often non-factual ideals, as Stephanie Coontz (2003) suggests in her work on American families and the 'myths' or our ideals that propel them along. Our participation in family life reflects the patterns we see in society: women tending to children, men tending to financial provision. Even in dual-income homes, most women perform a **second shift**, doing at least twice as much housework and childcare as their partners, because of their traditional role of caretakers in the home (see Bianchi, 2000; Coltrane, 2000). Women tend to wash clothes, clean, cook, shop for food and arrange for childcare; men tend to mow lawns, shovel snow, make household repairs and take out the trash. Regardless of careers, women still manage the domestic front and many see their usefulness in line with these tasks.

Family members create and maintain gendered paternal identities of mother and father through linguistic habits. Kendall (2006: 187) focuses on the 'display through positioning' that family members 'take up'. She sees that women use individualized topics over generalized topics when at home and in family conversations. Here's an example:

Elaine: Beth just really wants a dog, but uh

Richard: Oh yeah?

Elaine: Yeah.

Richard: Every kid does, I think. Most of them.

By referring to 'every kid', Richard generalizes the topic to connect with the world beyond family life, while Elaine has individualized the issue to focus on her own daughter only. Consequently, Elaine takes the parental position while Richard does not. He could have responded in the way he did even if he was not Beth's parent. Such patterns seem to align with gendered roles and expectations so that women stay focused on the particulars of their family members, while the masculine habit is to perceive of issues of life as beyond the immediacy of family members. Such a view is consistent with a difference perspective.

There are other linguistic tendencies which Kendall argues work in similar ways to position the mother as the one most responsible for child-rearing and the father in the role of breadwinner and less emotionally engaged with family members. Mothers often attempt to frame the conversations as symmetrical exchanges of family experiences, while fathers position themselves as less-engaged than mothers. In taking up the position of breadwinner, a man constructs a work identity and a greater commitment to life outside the home. Kendall sees tendencies with language as creating and reproducing gendered identities in line with work-related identities.

Drawing on a difference perspective then, women will often think in terms of closeness and support, and they focus to preserve intimacy in their personal relationships. Men tend to focus more on independence from family relationships. These traits can lead women and men to starkly different views of the same situation. Deborah Tannen (1991) gives the example of a woman who would check with her husband before inviting a guest to stay because she liked telling friends that she had to check with him (not because she really had to). Her husband, meanwhile, invited people over without consulting his wife because consulting her would mean a loss of his independent status. Such tendencies get rehearsed and performed throughout our lives as we move through various relationships: we behave in certain ways out of a need and desire to be perceived in certain ways by others. We project an image of ourselves that we believe will be positive and acceptable to those we care most about. This approval connects strongly with our genderedness and the gender we represent: we are approved of in highly gendered ways. This interpretation of gender and relationships suggests that our performance of such genderedness leads to an internalization of these traits: we become what we do.

Gender and friendships

Friendships allow us the opportunity to partake in relationships based on choice instead of kinship. By making friends, we assert our autonomy: we choose who to spend time with. The most blatant obstacle to female friendship is the prevailing patriarchal adage that 'women are their own worst enemies'. By promoting this view, we ensure that women will be each other's worst enemies. Valerie Hey (1996) says that the friendships of girls are sometimes affirming but often times sites of pain and betrayal. Because of internalized misogyny, girls and later women work against each other and compete for a whole host of successes, including male attention but also female friendship, fun and appearance. Janice Raymond (1985) sees that instead of engagement with more worldly concerns, women engage in an over-concern for their own lives and come to see any talk-therapy as 'a way of life'. Raymond's research points to ways women use talk at the center of their relationships as a form of therapy – 'a tyranny of feelings' – where women come to believe that what really counts in their life is their search for health and happiness and their ability to articulate this. Women use their friendships as therapy. A key way this therapeutic relationship is developed is through mutual self-disclosure. Women must show and tell all to each other. Raymond calls this a 'psychological strip-tease' that can fragment and exploit the inner life. The relationship-centeredness of many women makes other people the center of a woman's life, so that when a relationship ends, all else fails.

There has also been increased scholarly interest in boys' friendships and the role these play in establishing acceptable masculine identities. Boy culture appears to be established mainly through actions and shared activity (Pollack, 1998). According to this view, boys are particularly motivated to avoid shame and to increase their athletic ability. But researchers have also explored what boys and men talk about in their friendship groups, suggesting that boys often discuss similar topics to girls in their friendship groups, which interrupts certain claims of essential difference in this regard (Cameron, 1995; Coates, 2003).

Jennifer Coates (1996, 2004) has done a considerable amount of research on linguistic patterns in friendships. There are linguistic features in these friendships, such as: topic and topic introduction; latching; minimal response; hedging; questions; and turn-taking. These features are underpinned by Coates's belief that female speech (if it exists) is not weak but a style of speaking that is based on a goal of 'maintenance of good social relationships' (p. 139).

Coates admits that different conversational settings might require varying levels of competition over relationship-building speech patterns for both males and females. Female conversations may more often be relationship/community based even though 'the ideal (androgynous) speaker would be competent in both [settings]' (p. 139). Deborah Jones (1990) categorizes friendship discourse into four main themes:

- House talk: the exchange of information and resources connected with the female role as an occupation.
- Scandal: the talk about the behavior of others, and of women in particular. It is usually made in terms of the domestic morality of which women have been appointed guardians.
- Bitching: the overt expression of women's anger at their restricted roles or inferior status. They express this frustration in private and to other women only. The women who bitch are not expecting change; they want only to make their complaints in an environment where their anger will be understood and expected.
- Chatting: the most intimate form of gossip, a mutual self-disclosure, a transaction where women use to their own advantage the skills they have learned as a part of their job of nurturing others.

Such themes frame conversations in many female friendships so that they are the feminine 'scripts'. To not engage with these themes would exclude a woman from full connectedness. With her friendship network, a woman would utilize the themes of house talk, scandal, bitching and chatting to connect, affirm and protect the friendship. This social talk is the connective tissue for most women in their friendship groups.

One in-depth look at female friendships is Kate Fillion's (1996) book, *Lip Service*. It provides insights into how close girlfriends relate to one another and why men come in for so much criticism for not making friends in a similar way. The gist of it is that intimacy has been defined in a feminine way so that women come out as the *de facto* intimacy experts over men. Such ideas echo Tannen's and Gilligan's that self-disclosure is the defining feature of female intimacy – that women measure closeness by how much personal disclosure transpires. Julia Wood (1997) connects this idea to how men are judged to be less adept at intimacy because they fail to emphasize the personally disclosive talk that characterizes women's relationships.

In Wood's (1997) research, more men said that they demonstrate affection by doing things for and with others, but this activity-based frame got low ratings on intimacy scales from women. Women said they demonstrated affection by telling others about their feelings and they got higher ratings from women as a direct result. Men told researchers that they feel close to their friends through 'mutual give and take', 'helping each other out', 'being there' and 'sharing activities'. Women said that these demonstrations did not matter as much to them as self-disclosure did, declaring more masculine ways of connecting as less than meaningful.

Deborah Cameron (1995) says that wherever and whenever the matter has been investigated, both men and women have been found to face normative expectations about the appropriate mode of speech for their gender. Both men and women have been instructed and rehearsed (by each other) in the most acceptable ways of talking (just as they have been instructed in the most acceptable ways of dressing) to align with genderedness. Their acceptance of a 'proper' speech style is what Cameron describes as 'verbal hygiene'. Cameron claims that verbal hygiene is a way to make sense of language and represents a symbolic attempt to impose order on the social world. We belong because and when we play by the relevant gender rules.

Politeness and complimenting

Of relevance here is the work of Janet Holmes (1995, 2003) and her theory of politeness. Her data suggest that all people tend to be more polite to people who are socially superior, important to them, or strangers. Holmes connects women's experiences as often with those who are socially superior (such as with their bosses) or with strangers, if their lives pivot more around their home life. As such, women get more practice with polite talk on a daily basis.

Janet Holmes (1995) also puts forward the related theory of complimenting, identifying three types of compliments, namely: compliments related to appearance ('What a lovely dress'), compliments in the form of greetings ('How good to see you here') and expressions of concern ('You seem to be much stronger'). Holmes maintains that giving praise in these ways is inherently asymmetrical; the speaker is attempting to 'one-up' the other. Her data from TV talk shows indicates that women give 70% of compliments and receive about 75% of them. Compliments between men are rare – less than 10%. This discrepancy suggests that women are giving compliments to each other and, as a result, are recipients of all manner of social judgments. According to Holmes, the way a woman is spoken to is a subtle and powerful way of perpetuating her subordinate role in society. Like giving praise to a child, such complimenting can be patronizing.

Holmes' research explores how women are complimented on their appearance and behavior while men are more likely to be complimented on their abilities and possessions. She provides evidence of men being more likely to pay compliments to women of higher status. As such, Holmes sees women as complimented most by their equals and their peers and friends, as a way of connecting with each other and perhaps even to control each other for the purposes of self-affirmation. Also, female friendships in particular are complex sites where a feminine style of speaking (such as using backchannel support, latching, listening and so on) can 'ghettoize' women, inadvertently limiting a wider worldview. Women connect with each other through conversation but, within these conversations, women use language to narrow the focus onto personal lives rather than outside issues. Their friendships serve as both sites of support, but also sites of exclusion.

Rosalind Wiseman (2002) explored the pain at the center of many female friendships in adolescence in her book, *Queen Bees and Wannabees*. Here she explores the dynamics of peer groups and the power games that play out within them. Rachel Simmons (2002) also examines female friendships in her book, *Odd Girl Out*, and identifies the 'hidden aggression' inside female friendship groups. Because of such explorations, we can no longer view women as simply the nurturers: gender roles are too complex for these generalizations.

Talk used in personal relationships reveals both a social construction of gender as well as alignments of gendered patterns mainly in keeping with a difference perspective. Because the role of men in our society has been and continues to be work-based, these patterns are carried into personal relations at home and in friendship groups. Personal relationships are centered around feelings of belonging and of participation regardless of one's sex. How people behave in their personal relations seems to closely align with gender differentiated ways of communicating: women build rapport with others through conversations and men function as individuals more disengaged from personal relationships, but these tendencies often work against each other as are viewed from an assumption of difference.

Summary statements

- The gendered roles we play in our personal relationships are often revealed in linguistic practices; for example, women to tend to individualize topics while men tend to generalize and distance themselves from the context.

- Both women and men have been instructed and rehearsed into the acceptable ways of talking, just as they have been instructed in acceptable ways of dressing in order to align with a particular gender identity. We behave in certain ways because we are comfortable doing so.

Discussion points

With a partner or on your own, consider:

1. How is it helpful to consider in which ways talking functions in personal relationships?

2. If girls and women tend to participate in relationships with their main focus being on rapport and inclusion, and boys and men tend to focus their relationships on shared activity, what do these tendencies tell us?

3. What can we learn from the various gendered identities in our many family roles or in our friendship groups? Is there something girls and women can learn from a more masculine speech? Is there something boys and men can learn from feminine speech?

Further reading

To read more on gender, language and personal relationships, see:

Coates, J. (1996) *Women Talk: Conversation between Women Friends*. Oxford: Blackwell.

Coates, J. (2003) *Men Talk*. Oxford: Blackwell.

Connell, R. W. (2001) *Men and the Boys*. Los Angeles: University of California Press.

Coontz, S. (2003) *The Way We Never Were: American Families and the Nostalgia Trap*. New York: Basic Books.

Hey, V. (1996) *The Company She Keeps: An Ethnography of Girls' Friendship*. Buckingham: Open University Press.

Kendall, S. (2006) Positioning the female voice within work and family. In J. Baxter (ed.) *Speaking Out: The Female Voice in Public Contexts* (pp. 179–97). Basingstoke: Palgrave Macmillan.

Simmons, R. (2002) *Odd Girl Out: The Hidden Culture of Aggression in Girls*. Orlando, FL: Harcourt Books.

Wiseman, R. (2002) *Queen Bees and Wannabees: Helping Your Daughter Survive Gossip, Boyfriends, and Other Realities of Adolescence*. New York: Crown Publishers.

8

Looking to the future

As the final chapter, this section reflects on possible future areas of exploration in light of the field of gender and language studies to this point by asking these questions:

- How do we reconcile the uniqueness and complexity of individuals with the persistent language patterns seen along gendered lines?

- Why is it important not to essentialize gender or gendered patterns with language use?

- In what ways is globalization opening new sites of gender and language use? Is it that there is more to know or more evidence to gather?

- And finally, what new gender issues are yet to be explored?

'Women are not inherently passive or peaceful. [Women] are not inherently anything but human.'
Robin Morgan, American feminist (1941–)

Very broadly speaking, this book has focused on two different things:
1. how language reveals, represents, constructs and sustains attitudes to gender; and
2. how language users speak in ways that reveal and construct their genderedness.

Both of these include historic influences, past views of what makes a good woman or man, and a recognition that language is used to control or connect us in some way. Studying language can and must be objective insofar as we can assess, record and reflect on language. The issues are complex.

The issues of nature or nurture, or heredity/biology and environment, connect with education, family patterns and social conditioning. Each individual is a mysterious and unique combination of such factors. However, there seem to be some persistent patterns seen in the language along gendered lines. Studying gender and language is interesting in large part because we often want to find support for our developing views. It can be very easy to use the claims made by linguists in the past to explain our present circumstances, but such ventures are eventually unsatisfactory because research done in specific communities from the 1960s to the 1990s may not relate to our current circumstances. We are unique and special, but we also interconnect. The pulling on these threads is a major element to the field.

It is certainly important to caution all new scholars to the field against adopting entrenched positions or dismissing ideas if they shake up new views. Any attempt to divide the world into two sexes with no common ground is to be resisted. The world is complex and we, as participants in it, are not easily categorized or predictable, even while scholars offer some evidence to the contrary. It seems to me after a lifetime of reflection on the matter that more and more evidence always serves to complexify the relationship of gender and language use. This complexity is to be continually explored because it is continually changing.

Poverty and globalization

Of growing concern in the West is the issue of sustainable development and the role globalization has played in creating poverty. For those involved in gender studies, it is no secret that poverty is more often a women's issue, whether in the West or in the developing world. Most often, women and small farmers are the primary food providers in the world's poorest countries. Local diversity and sustainable food systems are being destroyed in the name of increasing global food production. Economic globalization is leading to increased debt around the world. In the regions where industrial agriculture has been introduced through globalization, higher costs are making it virtually impossible for people to survive. Estimates say that nearly one out of six people in this world (more than one billion people) are crossing national borders as migrant workers. Of these one billion, 72% are women. The work migrant workers do is usually poorly paid, low-status work that others are happy to pass on as an 'opportunity' for someone else. The two most common jobs are domestic or agricultural labor. Women and girls from all over the world are recruited as domestic workers. In North America and Europe, women from South America and Asia work in the homes of the rich sending money back home to their families abroad. Common experiences include low wages, long hours, loneliness, verbal abuse, racism and vulnerability to sexual abuse. Many domestic workers leave children and family behind in their home countries (Bakan & Stasiulis, 1997), while huge numbers of poverty-stricken girls and women accept the promise of a good job but find they have been tricked into and trapped by prostitution (Wichterich, 2000).

In studying language, it is helpful for us to consider that the consensus view is that gender makes some impact on the way we live out our lives. Equally, this impact is not universal and people make choices in various settings and for a variety of reasons to make meaning from their lives. I believe that we all have been rehearsed into our culture's gender performances and that the rehearsal is closely connected to language. We grow up inside families, communities, schools and particular cultures, ethnicities and worldviews. These elements all have an effect in our lives and the choices we make on a daily basis. We are influenced by those around us and we likewise influence those closest to us.

The field of sociolinguistics is concerned with how language connects with these choices. Would I still be myself if I were born male? How central is my sex to my gender identity? I think that, no, I would not be the person I am now if I had been born male: my life trajectory would be different because society would treat me differently. My being born female has influenced my early experiences with others. I am a daughter, sister, wife and mother, not a son, brother, husband or father. I am female, and not incidentally, I am viewed as feminine by the world around me.

The rise of feminism has opened up the lives of women to include connection to the world beyond family life. But this journey has not been quick or painless or necessarily beneficial. Many thinkers, philosophers, politicians and researchers have explored the boundaries of gender roles and gender tendencies that continue to surround both sexes and create such distinct life experiences in the workplace and in personal relationships. We are not from separate planets; we are here, on planet earth, all sharing its joys and responsibilities. We need the full range of gender identities to humanize our lived experiences. We are all capable of strength and responsiveness, both independence and interdependence, both competitiveness and collaboration.

It is my opinion, at least at the moment, that differences are not the problem in our lives. We live with who we are. What is a problem, and a problem worth engaging, is gender polarization and the tension between perceived differences. Perhaps we need to use other words rather than 'difference' (which creates and supports a binary), words like 'tapestry' of gender or 'symphony' of gender so as to better conceptualize gender identity as a mixture of various styles and purposes.

As stated at the beginning of this book, I wonder how much of an effect gender has had on my life choices, my self-concept and identity, and my relationships with others and how language plays a part. I can appreciate that socialization is powerful and insidious; but I also appreciate that we are all complex combinations of past and present situations.

I also wonder what kind of world do we want: a divided, ghettoized society or one where people are recognized to be worthwhile, regardless of gender, age, appearance, faith, color, class or sex? Our language use in the media, in education, in the workplace, in our faith communities and in our personal relationships matters a great deal in creating and then protecting a world we want.

There are many areas of inquiry I have not explored here, namely gender and language use in politics, in law, in sports, in psychological development, in aging or in various cultures around the world: there is much potential for important research in each. There is also so much more to say on the topics discussed in this book and so much more complexity to discuss. Nevertheless, I hope the topics introduced here have given you a sense of the field of gender and language use, along with some key notions and concepts within it.

Finally, I want to say that I continue to worry about how gender influences our lived experience. Women are the usual victims of domestic violence and abuse; women are more often than not the victims of the media's use of ideal images; older women are more despised than older men; women are still socialized to dependency and enmeshment, but men to autonomy and power. Around the world, women are victims of rape, prostitution and infanticide. In some places, women are the property of men; poverty is largely a women's issue. I am troubled by the ways our gender marks us and limits our possibilities. My ultimate hope is that your increased awareness of gender and language use will open up your own understandings of human connection, and that your own experiences will be fuller because of it. I wish you well.

Glossary

Androcentric
Describing the practice, conscious or otherwise, of placing male human beings or the masculine point of view at the center of one's view of the world and its culture and history.

Baby-boomers
Those born during any period of increased birth rate, but is particularly applied to those born during the post-World War II period and before the Vietnam War. In Europe, it is also known as the Generation of 1968.

Biological determinism
The hypothesis that biological factors such as one's individual genes (as opposed to social or environmental factors) completely determine how one behaves or changes over time. It is the opposite of social determinism.

Complementarian
A term to describe a Christian theological view that an unequal status of men and women, particularly in marriage and in Church leadership, is Biblically required. The term replaces what previously was known as the traditionalist view of gender relationships.

Consciousness raising groups
A form of political action pioneered by US radical feminists in the late 1960s. The groups of women aimed to get a better understanding of women's oppression by bringing women together to discuss and analyze their lives without interference from the presence of men.

Consumer femininity – *see Consumer gender*

Consumer gender
The study of how people buy, what they buy, when they buy, and why they buy in alignment with gender stereotypes and gender identity. It attempts to understand the buyer decision-making process in gender groupings.

Consumer masculinity – *see Consumer gender*

Critical Discourse Analysis (CDA)
An interdisciplinary approach to the study of discourse that views language as a form of social practice; it focuses on the ways social and political domination/power is reproduced by text and talk. The patterns of access to communicative events is an essential element of CDA.

Egalitarian
A term to describe the moral doctrine that people should be treated as equals. Generally it applies to being held equal under the law and the Church, particularly concerning gender roles and contributions.

Equal Rights Amendment
A proposed amendment to the United States Constitution that was intended to guarantee equal rights under the law for Americans regardless of sex, but it failed to pass Congress approval in both 1979 and again in 1982.

Essentialism
The view that, for any specific kind of entity, it is at least theoretically possible for there to be a set of characteristics all of which members of a specified group have.

Feminine/femininity
Refers to qualities and behaviors judged by a particular culture to be ideally associated with or especially appropriate to women and girls. In Western culture, femininity has traditionally included features such as gentleness and patience.

Gender
Refers to the social construction of behaviors in alignment with masculine or feminine behaviors, rather than the biological condition of maleness or femaleness. The term gender is often used interchangeably with sex in common usage but in the social sciences it refers to socioculturally adapted traits.

Gender bias – *see Sexism*

Gendered
To be made into masculine or feminine ways of behaving.

Gender-inclusive language (or gender-neutral language)
A description of language usages that are aimed at minimizing assumptions regarding the biological sex of human referents and are aimed at clarifying the inclusion of both sexes and genders.

Gender roles
A set of perceived behavioral norms associated particularly with males or females, in a given social group or system, and is often a focus for analysis in the social sciences. All societies have a gender/sex system, although the components and workings of this system vary widely from society to society.

(The) glass ceiling

Refers to situations where the advancement of a person within the hierarchy of an organization is limited. This limitation is usually based on either race or gender. 'Glass' refers to the limitation as not immediately apparent and is normally an unwritten or unofficial policy.

Hierarchy

A system of ranking and organizing things or people, where each element of the system (except for the top element) is subordinate to a single other element. In gender studies, the hierarchy is usually understood as being male dominated and female subordinated.

Ideal

A principle or value that one actively pursues as a goal. In gender studies, the ideal is the gendered values supported by any given society or group.

Liberal feminism

A form of feminism that argues that equality for women can be achieved through legal means and social reform, and that men as a group need not be challenged. Liberal feminism leans towards an equality of sameness with men.

Linguistic space

This is the amount of talking taken up by a speaker or speakers in any given conversation. One can take a lot of linguistic space by saying a lot, while another may take very little linguistic space by not saying much out loud.

Masculine/masculinity

Refers to qualities and behaviors judged by a particular culture to be ideally associated with or especially appropriate to men. In Western culture, masculinity has traditionally included features such as strength and independence.

Minorities

Groups that do not constitute a politically dominant set of the total population of a given society. A sociological minority is not necessarily a numerical minority; it may include any group that is disadvantaged with respect to a dominant group in terms of social status, education, employment, wealth and political power.

Misogyny

Hatred or strong prejudice against women as a group and femininity in general. It is often a political ideology that justifies and maintains the subordination of women to men.

National Organization of Women (NOW)

An American feminist group founded in 1966 with currently over 500,000 contributing members. During the 1970s in particular, NOW promoted the Equal Rights Amendment to the US Constitution.

Normative/the norm

The term used to describe the effects of those structures of culture that regulate the function of social activity. Normative also describes actions intended to normalize something or to make it acceptable.

(The) other – or othering

A key concept that refers to that which is other than oneself. The concept of otherness is integral to the understanding of identities, as people construct roles for themselves in relation to an 'other'.

Othering – *see (The) other*

Patriarchy

The structuring of society on the basis of family units in which fathers have primary responsibilities for the welfare of their families and, by extension, the responsibility for the community as a whole. There are no known examples of matriarchies from any point in history.

Power

From the French word *pouvoir*, meaning 'to be able'. Power is more or less unilateral ability (either real or perceived) or potential to bring about significant change through the actions of oneself or of others. The term 'power' is contested by scholars because of the assumptions surrounding who or what has it.

Racism

Bigotry, prejudice, violence, oppression, stereotyping, discrimination or any other socially divisive practice whose primary basis is the concept of race. It is also the belief or ideology that all members of each race possess characteristics of abilities specific to that race, especially to distinguish it as being either superior or inferior to another.

Radical feminism

A branch of feminism that views women's oppression as a basic system of power upon which human relationships in society are arranged and seeks to challenge this arrangement by rejecting standard gender roles. Radical feminists locate the root cause of women's oppression in patriarchal gender relations, as opposed to legal systems (liberal feminism) or class conflict (socialist feminism).

Sapir–Whorf hypothesis

An axiom underlying the work of Edward Sapir and Benjamin Whorf in the 1920s that states that there is a systematic relationship between the language a person speaks and how that person both understands the world and behaves in it. The nature of a particular language influences the habitual thought of its speakers.

Second shift

In two-career couples, men and women on average spend about equal amounts of time working, but women still spend more time on housework (known as her 'second shift'). Several studies provide statistical evidence that married men contribute a smaller share of housework, regardless of whether or not they earn more than their wives.

Sex

Referring to the male and female duality of biology and reproduction. Also a contested term.

Sex differences

A distinction of biological and/or physiological characteristics typically associated with either males or females of a species in general. For example, on average men are taller than women, but an individual woman may be taller than an individual man.

Sexism

The discrimination and/or hatred against people based on their sex rather than their individual merits. It can also refer to any and all systemic differentiations based on the sex of the individuals.

Social sciences

A group of academic disciplines that study human aspects of the world. They tend to emphasize the use of the scientific method in the study of humanity, including quantitative and qualitative methods. Usually (but not always) the social sciences include: anthropology, economics, education, geography, law, linguistics, politics, philosophy, psychology and sociology.

Socialist feminism

A branch of feminism that focuses upon both the public and private sphere of a woman's life and argues that liberation can only be achieved by working to end both the economic and cultural sources of women's oppression.

Socially constructed

Any institutionalized entity or artifact in a social system where the meaning is constructed by participation in a particular culture or society that exists because people agree to behave according to conventional rules.

Subjectivity

Refers to the property of perceptions, arguments and language as being based in a subject's point of view, and hence influenced in accordance with a particular bias and related to power relations. Its opposite property is objectivity, which refers to such as based in a separate, distant and unbiased point of view.

Synthetic sisterhood

The process by which writings treat their mass audience as if they were individuals. Using linguistic devices, such as personal pronouns and presuppositions, magazines or newspapers or other media construct a simulated friendship between audience member and the producer. Sometimes called synthetic personalization.

Theory of deficit or dominance/dominance theory

The theory that states that societies are stratified by sex and that human social hierarchies consist of a hegemonic group at the top, usually men; and that women are dominated by the power of those born male.

Theory of difference/difference theory

The theory postulating that there are innate or socialized differences in the use of language between males and females.

Voice

Refers to the authenticity and distinctiveness of someone's spoken or written expression and aligns with the right, opportunity or ability to express a choice or opinion.

Bibliography

AAUWEF (1992) *Shortchanging Girls/Shortchanging America*. Washington DC: American Association of University Women Educational Foundation.

Alanti, C. (1995) Primary school teachers' expectations of boys' disruptiveness in the classroom: A gender-specific aspect of the hidden curriculum. In S. Mills (ed.) *Language and Gender: Interdisciplinary Perspectives* (pp. 149–59). Harlow: Addison Wesley Longman.

Andres, L. and Krahn, H. (1999) Youth pathways in articulated post-secondary systems: Enrollment and completion patterns of urban young men and women. *Canadian Journal of Higher Education* 29 March (1), 47–81.

Arquette, R. (Writer and Director) (2002) *Searching for Debra Winger*. [Motion Picture] USA: Immortal Entertainment.

Bailey, K. (1993) *The Girls are the Ones with the Pointy Nails*. London, Ontario: Althouse Press.

Bakan, A. and Stasiulis, D. (1997) *Not One of the Family: Domestic Workers in Canada*. Toronto: University of Toronto Press.

Baxter, J. (1999) Teaching girls to speak out: The female voice in public contexts. *Language and Education* 16 (2), 81–96.

Baxter, J. (2003) *Positioning Gender in Discourse: A Feminist Methodology*. Basingstoke: Palgrave Macmillan.

Baxter, J. (ed.) (2006) *Speaking Out: The Female Voice in Public Contexts*. Basingstoke: Palgrave Macmillan.

Bergvall, V. L. (1999) Toward a comprehensive theory of language and gender. *Language in Society* 28, 273–93.

Bianchi, S. (2000) Maternal employment and time with children: Dramatic change or surprising continuity? *Demography* November 37 (4), 401–14.

Bodine, A. (1975) Androcentrism in prescriptive grammar: Singular 'they,' sex-indefinite 'he,' and 'he or she.' *Language in Society* 4: 129–46.

Bourdieu, P. (1992) *Language and Symbolic Power*. Cambridge: Polity Press.

Bourdieu, P. (2001) *Masculine Domination*. Stanford, CA: Stanford University Press.

Brown, P. and Levinson, S. (1987) *Politeness: Some Universals in Language Usage*. Cambridge: Cambridge University Press.

Bucholtz, M. and Hall, K. (2004) Theorizing identity in language and sexuality research. *Language in Society* 33: 469–515.

Burn, E. (1989) Inside the lego house. In C. Skelton (ed.) *Whatever Happens to Little Women? Gender and Primary Schooling* (pp. 139–48). Milton Keyes: Open University Press.

Busse, C. (1998) Evangelical women in the 1990s: Examining internal dynamics. MA thesis, Briercrest Bible Seminary, Saskatchewan.

Butler, J. (1990) *Gender Trouble: Feminism and the Subversion of Identity*. London: Routledge.

Caldas-Coulthard, C. (1995) Man in the news: The misrepresentation of women in the news-as-narrative discourse. In S. Mills (ed.) *Language and Gender: Interdisciplinary Perspectives* (pp. 226–39) Harlow: Longman.

Cameron, D. (1995) *Verbal Hygiene*. London: Routledge.

Cameron, D. (ed.) (1998) *The Feminist Critique of Language* (2nd edn). London: Routledge.

Cameron, D. (2001) *Working with Spoken Discourse*. London: Sage.

Cameron, D. (2005) Language, gender and sexuality: Current issues and new directions. *Applied Linguistics* 26 (4), 482–502.

Cameron, D. (2007) *The Myth of Mars and Venus: Do Men and Women Really Speak Different Languages?* Oxford: Oxford University Press.

Cameron, D. and Kulick, D. (2003) *Language and Sexuality*. Cambridge: Cambridge University Press.

Carson, D. A. (1998) *The Inclusive-Language Debate: A Plea for Realism*. Grand Rapids, MI: Baker Books.

Cheshire, J. (2000) The telling or the tale? Narratives and gender in adolescent friendship networks. *Journal of Sociolinguistics* 4, 236–62.

Chopp, R. (1989) *The Power to Speak: Feminism, Language and God*. New York: Crossroad.

Coates, J. (1993) *Women, Men and Language* (2nd edn). New York: Longman.

Coates, J. (1996) *Women Talk: Conversation between Women Friends*. Oxford: Blackwell.

Coates, J. (1998) Gossip revisited: Language in all-female groups. In J. Coates (ed.) *Language and Gender: A Reader* (pp. 226–53). Oxford: Blackwell.

Coates, J. (2003) *Men Talk*. Oxford: Blackwell.

Coates, J. (2004) *Women, Men and Language* (3rd edn). New York: Pearson.

Coltrane, S. (2000) Research on household labor: Modeling and measuring the social embeddedness of routine family work. *Journal of Marriage and the Family* November 62 (4), 1208–33.

Connell, R. (1995) *Masculinities*. Cambridge: Polity.

Coontz, S. (2003) *The Way We Never Were: American Families and the Nostalgia Trap*. New York: Basic Books.

Corson, D. (1993) *Language, Minority Education and Gender: Linking Social Justice and Power*. Clevedon: Multilingual Matters.

Crawford, M. (1995) *Talking Difference: On Gender and Language*. London: Sage.

Daly, M. (1973) *The Church and the Second Sex*. New York: Harper and Row.

Davies, B. (1993) *Shards of Glass*. Sydney: Allen and Unwin.

Davies, J. (2003) Expressions of gender: An analysis of pupils' gendered discourse styles in small group discussions. *Discourse and Society* 14 (2), 115–32.

De Beauvoir, S. (1952) *The Second Sex*. New York: Vintage Books.

De Francisco, V. (1991) The sounds of silence: How men silence women in marital relations. *Discourse and Society* 2 (4), 413–23.

Delamont, S. (1990) *Sex Roles and the School* (2nd edn). London: Routledge.

Doriani, D. (2003) *Women and Ministry*. Wheaton, IL: Crossway Books.

Dworkin, A. (1981) *Pornography: Men Possessing Women*. Toronto: Women's Press.

Eckert, P. (1989) The whole woman: Sex and gender differences in variation. *Language Variation and Change* 1, 245–67.

Eckert, P. and McConnell-Ginet, S. (2003) *Language and Gender*. Cambridge: Cambridge University Press.

Edelsky, C. (1981) Who's got the floor? *Language in Society* 10 (3), 383–422.

Ehrlich, S. (2001) *Representing Rape: Language and Sexual Consent*. New York: Routledge.

Epstein, D., Elwood, J., Hey, V. and Maw, J. (eds) (1998) *Failing Boys? Issues in Gender and Achievement*. Buckingham: Open University Press.

Fairclough, N. (1989) *Language and Power*. London: Longman.

Fairclough, N. (1992) *Discourse and Social Change*. Cambridge: Polity Press.

Fairclough, N. (1995) *Media Discourse*. London: Arnold.

Faludi, S. (1993) *Backlash: The Undeclared War Against Women*. New York: Vintage.

Ferguson, M. (1983) *Forever Feminine: Women's Magazines and the Cult of Femininity*. London: Heinemann.

Fillion, K. (1996) *Lip Service: The Myth of Female Virtue in Love, Sex and Friendship*. New York: Harper Collins.

Fishman, P. (1980) Conversational insecurity. In H. Giles, W. P. Robinson and P. Smith (eds) *Language: Social Psychological Perspectives* (pp. 127–32). Oxford: Pergamon Press.

Fishman, P. (1983) Interaction: The work women do. In B. Thorne, C. Kramarae and N. Henley (eds) *Language, Gender and Society*. Rowley, MA: Newbury House.

Flanders, N. (1970) *Analyzing Teacher Behavior*. Reading, MA: Addison-Wesley.

Foucault, M. (1972) *The Archaeology of Knowledge and Discourse on Language*. New York: Pantheon Books.

Foucault, M. (1978) *The History of Sexuality: An Introduction*. Harmondsworth: Penguin.

Francis, B. (2000) The gendered subject: Students' preferences and discussions of gender and subject ability. *Oxford Review of Education* 26, 35–48.

Frazier, N. and Sadker, M. (1973) *Sexism in School and Society*. New York: Harper.

Freed, A. (1996) Language and gender in an experimental setting. In V. Bergall, J. Bing, and A. Freed (eds) *Rethinking Language and Gender Research: Theory and Practice* (pp. 54–76). New York: Longman.

Furlong, M. (1991) *A Dangerous Delight: Women and Power in the Church*. London: SPCK.

Gal, S. (1991) Between speech and silence: The problematics of research on language and gender. *Papers in Pragmatics* 3 (1), 1–38.

Gal, S. (1995) Language, gender and power: An anthropological review. In K. Hall and M. Bucholtz (eds) *Gender Articulated* (pp. 169–82). New York: Routledge.

Gallagher, S. K. (2003) *Evangelical Identity and Gendered Family Life*. London: Rutgers University Press.

Gauntlett, D. (2002) *Media, Gender and Identity: An Introduction*. New York: Routledge.

Gilligan, C. (1982) *In a Different Voice: Psychological Theory and Women's Development*. Cambridge, MA: Harvard University Press.

Goldberger, N. (1997) Ways of knowing. Does gender matter? In M. R. Walsh (ed.) *Women, Men, and Gender* (pp. 252–60). New Haven: Yale University Press.

Graddol, D. and Swann, J. (1989) *Gender Voices*. London: Blackwell.

Gray, J. (1994) *Men are from Mars, Women are from Venus: A Practical Guide for Improving Communication and Getting What You Want*. New York: Harper Collins.

Grenz, S. and Kjesbo, D. M. (1995) *Women in the Church*. Downers Grove, IL: Intervarsity Press.

Griffith, R. M. (1997) *God's Daughters: Evangelical Women and the Power of Submission*. Berkeley: University of California.

Gurian, M. and Stevens, K. (2005) *The Minds of Boys: Saving Our Sons from Falling Behind in School and Life*. San Francisco: Jossey-Bass Publishers.

Hall, K. and Bucholtz, M. (eds) (1995) *Gender Articulated Language and the Socially Constructed Self*. Oxford: Oxford University Press.

Hall, S. Chrichter, C., Jefferson, T., Clarke, J. and Roberts, B. (1978) *Policing the Crisis: Mugging, the State and Law and Order*. London: Macmillan.

Hancock, M. (ed.) (2003) *Christian Perspectives on Gender, Sexuality, and Community*. Vancouver: Regent College Publishing.

Helgesen, S. (1995) *The Female Advantage*. New York: Doubleday.

Herrett-Skjellum, J. and Allen, M. (1996) Television programming and sex-stereotyping: A meta-analysis. *Communication Yearbook* 19, 157–85.

Hey, V. (1996) *The Company She Keeps: An Ethnography of Girls' Friendship*. Buckingham: Open University Press.

Holmes, J. (1995) *Women, Men and Politeness*. London: Longman.

Holmes, J. (1998) Women's talk: The question of sociolinguistic universals. In J. Coates (ed.) *Language and Gender: A Reader* (pp. 461–83). Oxford: Blackwell.

Holmes, J. (2000) Politeness, power and provocation: Humour functions in the workplace. *Discourse Studies* 2 (2), 159–85.

Holmes, J. (2003) *Power and Politeness in the Workplace*. London: Longman.

Holmes, J. (2006) *Gendered Talk at Work*. Oxford: Blackwell.

Holmes, J. and Meyerhoff, M. (1999) The community of practice: Theories and methodologies in language and gender research. *Language in Society* 28, 173–83.

Ingersoll, J. (2003) *Evangelical Christian Women: War Stories in the Gender Battles*. New York: New York University Press.

Jaworski, A. (1993) *The Power of Silence*. London: Sage.

Jespersen, O. (1922) *Language. Its Nature, Development and Origin*. London: Allen & Unwin.

Jones, C. and Mahony, P. (eds) (1989) *Learning Our Lines: Sexuality and Social Control in Education*. London: Women's Press.

Jones, D. (1990) Gossip: Notes on women's oral culture. In D. Cameron (ed.) *The Feminist Critique of Language* (pp. 242–50). New York: Routledge.

Jule, A. (2004) *Gender and Silence in a Language Classroom: Sh-shushing the Girls*. Basingstoke: Palgrave Macmillan.

Jule, A. (ed.) (2005) *Gender and the Language of Religion*. Basingstoke: Palgrave Macmillan.

Jule, A. (2006) Silence as femininity?: A look at performances of gender theology college classrooms. In A. Jule and B. Pedersen (eds) *Being Feminist, Being Christian: Essays from Academia* (pp. 35–58). New York: Palgrave Macmillan.

Jule, A. (ed.) (2007) *Language and Religious Identity: Women in Discourse*. Basingstoke: Palgrave Macmillan.

Kendall, S. (2004) Framing authority: Gender, face and mitigation at a radio network. *Discourse and Society* 15, 55–79.

Kendall, S. (2006) Positioning the female voice within work and family. In J. Baxter (ed.) *Speaking Out: The Female Voice in Public Contexts* (pp. 179–97). Basingstoke: Palgrave Macmillan.

Kendall, S. and Tannen, D. (1997) Gender and language in the workplace. In R. Wodak (ed.) *Gender and Discourse* (pp. 81–105). New York: Longman.

Kilbourne, J. (2000) *Can't Buy My Love: How Advertising Changes the Way We Think and Feel*. Washington, DC: Free Press.

Kindlon, D. and Thompson, M. (1999) *Raising Cain: Protecting the Emotional Life of Boys*. New York: Ballentine Books.

Kramarae, C. and Treichler, P. (1990) Power relationships in the classroom. In S. Gabriel and I. Smithson (eds) *Gender in the Classroom: Power and Pedagogy* (pp. 41–59). Chicago: University of Illinois Press.

Kramarae, C., Treichler, P. and Russo, A. (1996) *A Feminist Dictionary*. London: Rivers Oram Press.

Labov, W. (1966) *The Social Stratification of English in New York City*. Washington DC: Center for Applied Linguistics.

Lacan, J. (1968) *The Language of the Self: The Function of Language in Psychoanalysis* (A. Wilden, trans.). Baltimore: Johns Hopkins University Press.

Lakoff, R. (1975) *Language and Woman's Place*. New York: Harper and Row.

Lakoff, R. (1995) Cries and whispers: The shattering of silence. In K. Hall and M. Bucholtz (eds) *Gender Articulated: Language and the Socially Constructed Self* (pp. 25–50). London: Routledge.

Lave, J. and Wenger, E. (1991) *Situated Learning: Legitimate Peripheral Participation*. Cambridge: Cambridge University Press.

Lazar, M. (ed.) (2005) *Feminist Critical Discourse Analysis: Studies in Gender, Power and Ideology*. London: Palgrave Macmillan.

Levy, A. (2005) *Female Chauvinist Pigs: Women and the Rise of Raunch Culture*. New York: Free Press.

Litosseliti, L. (2006) *Gender and Language: Theory and Practice*. London: Arnold.

Mac an Ghaill, M. (2000) The cultural production of English masculinities in late modernity. *Canadian Journal of Education* 25 (2), 88–101.

Maccoby, E. E. (1990) Gender and relationships: A developmental account. *American Psychologist* 45 (4), 513–20.

Mahony, P. (1985) *Schools for the Boys? Co-education Reassessed*. London: Hutchinson.

Maltz, D. N. and Borker, R. A. (1998) A cultural approach to male-female miscommunication. In J. Coates (ed.) *Language and Gender: A Reader* (pp. 417–34). Oxford: Blackwell.

Mannes, M. (1964) *But Will it Sell?* Philadelphia: Lippincott Press.

McConnell-Ginet, S. (2000) Breaking through the glass ceiling: Can linguistic awareness help? In J. Holmes (ed.) *Gendered Speech in Social Context: Perspectives from Gown to Town* (pp. 259–82). Wellington: Victoria University Press.

McElhinny, B. (1998) 'I don't smile much anymore.' In J. Coates (ed.) *Language and Gender: A Reader* (pp. 309–27). Oxford: Blackwell.

McRobbie, A. (1994) Folk devils fight back. *New Left Review* (203), 107–16.

Meyerhoff, M. (2005) Forward. In A. Jule (ed.) *Gender and the Language of Religion* (pp. x–xi). Basingstoke: Palgrave Macmillan.

Meyerhoff, M. (2006) *Introducing Sociolinguistics*. London: Routledge.

Mills, S. (ed.) (1995) *Language and Gender: Interdisciplinary Perspectives*. New York: Longman.

Mills, S. (2003a) *Gender and Politeness*. Cambridge: Cambridge University Press.

Mills, S. (2003b) Third wave feminist linguistics and the analysis of sexism. *Discourse Analysis Online*, www.extra.shu.ac.uk.

Mintzberg, H. (1973) *The Nature of Managerial Work*. New York: Harper & Row.

Mullany, L. (2003) Identity and role construction: A sociolinguistic study of gender and discourse in management. Unpublished PhD thesis, Nottingham Trent University, UK.

Mutch, B. H. (2003) Women in the church: A North American perspective. In M. Hancock (ed.) *Christian Perspectives on Gender, Sexuality, and Community* (pp. 181–93). Vancouver: Regent College Press.

Myers, G. (1994) *Words in Ads*. London: Arnold.

Myers, G. (1998) *Ad Worlds: Brands, Media, Audiences*. London: Arnold.

Nichols, P. (1983) Linguistic options and choices for women in the rural south. In B. Thorne, C. Kramarae and N. Henley (eds) *Language, Gender and Society* (pp. 54–68). Rowley, MA: Newbury House.

Oakley, A. (1972) *Gender and Society*. London: Temple Smith.

O'Barr, W. and Atkins, B. (1998) 'Women's language' or 'powerless language'? In J. Coates (ed.) *Language and Gender: A Reader* (pp. 377–87). Oxford: Blackwell.

Oxford, R. (1994) La difference ...: Gender differences in a second/foreign language learning styles and strategies. In J. Sunderland (ed.) *Exploring Gender: Questions and Implications for English Language Education* (pp. 140–7). New York: Prentice Hall.

Paechter, C. (1998) *Educating the Other: Gender, Power and Schooling*. London: Falmer.

Pauwels, A. (1998) *Women Changing Language*. New York: Longman.

Pavlenko, A. and Piller, I. (2001) Introduction. In A. Pavlenko, A. Blackledge, I. Piller and M. Teutsch-Dwyer (eds) *Multilingualism, Second Language Learning and Gender* (pp. 1–52). Berlin: Mouton de Gruyter.

Peters, M. (2007) The math on miss motor mouth. *Psychology Today* March/April, 21.

Pipher, M. (1994) *Reviving Ophelia: Saving the Souls of Adolescent Girls*. New York: Ballentine Books.

Pollack, W. (1998) *Real Boys: Rescuing our Sons from the Myths of Boyhood*. New York: Henry Holt & Co.

Rafelman, R. (1997) The party line. *Toronto Life*. November.

Raymond, J. (1985) *A Passion for Friends: Towards a Philosophy of Female Affection*. Boston: Beacon Press.

Reskin, B. and Roos, P. (eds) (1990) *Job Queues, Gender Queues: Explaining Women's Inroads Into Male Occupations*. Philadelphia: Temple University Press.

Reuther, R. R. (1998) *Introducing Redemption in Christian Feminism*. Sheffield: Sheffield Academic Press.

Sadker, M. and Sadker, D. (1985) Sexism in the schoolroom of the '80s. *Psychology Today* March, 54–7.

Sadker, M. and Sadker, D. (1990) Confronting sexism in the college classroom. In S. Gabriel and I. Smithson (eds) *Gender in the Classroom: Power and Pedagogy* (pp. 176–87). Chicago: University of Illinois Press.

Sapir, E. (1929) The status of linguistics as a science. In E. Sapir (1958) *Culture, Language and Personality* (D.G. Madelbaum, ed.). Berkeley: University of California Press.

Scanzoni, L. D. (1966) Women's place: Silence or service? *Eternity* 17 (February), 14–16.

Sheldon, A. (1997) Talking power: Girls, gender enculturation and discourse. In R. Wodak (ed.) *Gender and Discourse* (pp. 225–44). London: Sage.

Short, G. and Carrington, B. (1990) Discourses on gender: The perspectives of children aged six and eleven. In C. Skelton (ed.) *Whatever Happens to Little Women?: Gender and Primary Schooling* (pp. 22–37). Milton Keyes: Open University Press.

Simmons, R. (2002) *Odd Girl Out: The Hidden Culture of Aggression in Girls*. Orlando, FL: Harcourt Books.

Skelton, C. (2001) *Schooling the Boys: Masculinities and Primary Education*. Buckingham: Open University Press.

Smith, S. L. (2006a) *G Movies Give Boys a D: Portraying Males as Dominant, Disconnected and Dangerous*.

Program Brief, *See Jane* Program at Dads and Daughters. May, www.seejane.org.

Smith, S. L. (2006b). *Where the Girls Aren't: Gender Disparity Saturates G-Rated Films*. Program Brief, *See Jane* Program at Dads and Daughters. February, www.seejane.org.

Spender, D. (1980) *Man Made Language*. London: Pandora.

Spender, D. (1982) *Invisible Women: The Schooling Scandal*. London: Writers and Readers Publishing Corp.

Spender, D. (1990) *Women of Ideas: And What Men Have Done To Them*. Toronto: Harper Collins Canada.

Spender, D. and Sarah, E. (1980) *Learning to Lose: Sexism and Education*. London: The Women's Press.

Stanworth, M. (1983) *Gender and Schooling: A Study of Sexual Divisions in the Classroom*. London: Hutchinson.

Storkey, E. (2001) *Origins of Difference: The Gender Debate Revisited*. Grand Rapids, MI: Baker Book House Company.

Sunderland, J. (1998) Girls being quiet: A problem for foreign language classrooms. *Language Teaching Research* 2 (1), 48–62.

Sunderland, J. (2004) *Gendered Discourses*. Basingstoke: Palgrave.

Swann, J. (1992) *Girls, Boys, and Language*. Oxford: Blackwell.

Swann, J. (1998) Talk control: An illustration from the classroom of problems in analysing male dominance of conversation. In J. Coates (ed.) *Language and Gender: A Reader* (pp. 185–96). Oxford: Blackwell.

Swann, J. and Graddol, D. (1995) Feminising classroom talk? In S. Mills (ed.) *Language and Gender: Interdisciplinary Perspectives* (pp. 135–48). Harlow: Addison Wesley Longman.

Szirom, T. (1988) *Teaching Gender?: Sex Education and Sexual Stereotypes*. Sydney: Allen and Unwin.

Talbot, M. (1995) A synthetic sisterhood: False friends in a teenage magazine. In K. Hall and M. Bucholtz (eds) *Gender Articulated: Language and the Socially Constructed Self* (pp. 143–68). New York: Routledge.

Talbot, M. (1998) *Language and Gender: An Introduction*. Cambridge: Polity Press.

Tannen, D. (1991) *You Just Don't Understand: Women and Men in Conversation*. New York: William Morrow.

Tannen, D. (1995) *Talking from 9 to 5*. London: Virago.

Tannen, D. (1998) *The Argument Culture*. London: Virago.

Thomas, L. (1996) Invisible women: Gender and the exclusive language debate. In S. Porter (ed.) *The Nature of Religious Language: A Colloquium* (pp. 159–69). Sheffield: Sheffield University Press.

Thornborrow, J. (2002) *Power Talk*. London: Longman.

Today's New International Version (2002) *The Bible*. Grand Rapids, MI: Zondervan Publishing.

Trudgill, P. (1974) *Sociolinguistics: An Introduction*. Harmondsworth: Penguin.

Valpy, M. (2007) Are Anglicans facing a great schism? *Globe and Mail*, March 19, A3.

Walkerdine, V. (1990) *Schoolgirl Fictions*. London: Versco.

Walsh, C. (2001) *Gender and Discourse: Language and Power in Politics, the Church and Organizations*. London: Pearson Education.

Walsh, M. R. (ed.) (1997) *Women, Men and Gender: Ongoing Debates*. New Haven: Yale University Press.

West, C. (1984) *Routine Complications: Trouble with Talk between Doctors and Patients*. Bloomington: Indiana University Press.

West, C. (1990) Not just 'doctors' orders': Directive-response sequences in patients' visits to women and men physicians. *Discourse and Society* 1 (1), 85–112.

West, C. and Zimmerman, D. (1987) Doing gender. *Gender and Society* 1, 125–51.

Wichterich, C. (2000) *The Globalized Woman: Reports from a Future of Inequality*. New York: Zed Books.

Wiseman, R. (2002) *Queen Bees and Wannabees: Helping Your Daughter Survive Gossip, Boyfriends, and Other Realities of Adolescence*. New York: Crown Publishers.

Wodak, R. (ed.) (1997) *Gender and Discourse*. London: Sage.

Women's Media: The Site for Working Women (2003) www.womensmedia.com.

Wood, J. (1997) Clarifying the issues. *Personal Relationships* 4 (3), 221–8.

Woolf, V. (1928) *A Room of One's Own*. London: Penguin.

Yates, L. (1997) Gender, equity and the boys debate: What sort of challenge is it? *British Journal of Sociology of Education* 18 (3), 337–47.

Younger, M., Warrington, M. and Williams J. (1999) The gender gap and classroom interactions: Realities and rhetoric. *British Journal of Sociology in Education* 20 (3), 325–41.

Zimmerman, D. and West, C. (1975) Sex roles, interruptions and silences in conversation. In B. Thorne and V. Henley (eds) *Language and Sex: Difference and Dominance* (pp. 105–29). Rowley, MA: Newbury House.

Index